REINTERPRETING GENOESE CIVIL CONFLICTS

REINTERPRETING GENOESE CIVIL CONFLICTS

The Chronicle of Ottobonus Scriba

by
Agostino Inguscio

Quid Pro Books
New Orleans, Louisiana

Copyright © 2015 by Agostino Inguscio. All rights reserved. The author's intellectual property and moral rights are further asserted.

Published in 2015 by Quid Pro Books, as part of the *History & Heroes* Series.

ISBN 978-1-61027-285-8 (paperback)
ISBN 978-1-61027-305-3 (hardcover)
ISBN 978-1-61027-304-6 (ebook)

QUID PRO BOOKS
5860 Citrus Blvd., Suite D-101
New Orleans, Louisiana 70123
www.quidprobooks.com

qp

Publisher's Cataloging-in-Publication

Inguscio, Agostino
 Reinterpreting Genoese Civil Conflicts: The Chronicle of Ottobonus Scriba / Agostino Inguscio.
  p. cm. — (History & heroes)
 Includes bibliographical references.
 ISBN: 978-1-61027-285-8 (pbk.)
1. Europe—History—476–1492. 2. Italy—Genoa. 3. Italy—Social conditions. 4. Italy—Commerce—History. I. Title. II. Series.

HF3584.I23 2015   357.91'59—dc22
                                          2015737252

Cover image is part of a painting entitled "Grande blu," 2010, by Giovanna Rasario, *www.rasario.it*, copyright © 2010 by the artist. The author and publisher thank her for sharing this remarkable work for this project. Author photograph on back cover inset depicts the author in archives in Genoa, November 2014, copyright © 2014, used by permission. Other images derive from public domain sources.

CONTENTS

Foreword i
Preface v
Acknowledgements vii

Introduction 1
1 • Sources Utilised 7
2 • A Crescendo Ground Noise of Conflicts, 1174-1189 15
3 • An Escalation in Civil Conflicts and an
    Institutional Evolution 31
4 • A Critique of the Recent Literature and a
    Possible Economics of Conflict 41
Conclusion 59
Afterword 61

Bibliography 71
Appendix 81
About the Author 89

Foreword
Bringing History Back In

Why should a political sociologist comment and introduce the work of an economic historian? The answer is rather simple but of incredible importance: the interest in Agostino Inguscio's account of civil conflict in Medieval Genoa goes beyond the study of a medieval town in the 11th and 12th century. The challenge he proposes to Greif's rational choice theory based explanation of Genoese political and institutional change is both substantial and theoretical in tone. Substantively, Inguscio's evidence contests and contradicts Greif's conclusion on numerous grounds. One cannot ignore Genoa had already decided to elect a *podestà* before an external threat to the political stability of the city materialised. Theoretically, Inguscio seriously questions Greif's working method. The economist confused hypothesis and empirical testing in order to generalise a theoretical frame that clearly does not seem to apply to Medieval Genoa.

The work of this young and promising historian implicitly approaches a widespread bias in social science: the simplistic use of history to demonstrate a theory. Greif's attempt to superimpose rational choice theory to a context that did not function according to this logic is yet an example of the domination of economics over other social sciences and history. Greif's explanation reminds me a lot of another example of a flawed analysis of Italian history: Putnam's explanation of social capital shortage in the South of Italy. The American scholar, in a very deterministic manner, suggested the origin of the lack of social capital in the *Mezzogiorno* has to be found in the despotic rule of Frederick the second (the same historical period Inguscio takes into account to shed a light on Genoese civil conflict).

Reinterpreting Genoese Civil Conflicts

However, Putnam, as much as Greif, ignored many historical events and documents that pointed in a different direction.

More generally, the dismissal of the idea of history as a perpetual problem solving exercise of human kind (Fukuyama 1992; Putnam 1993) is contributing to the generation of deterministic theories and visions of the world. Such determinism has indeed reduced the heuristic potential of history to a pre-established path to modernity, as exemplified by Putnam's and Greif's work. In this book, Inguscio proposes the best antidote against this widely spread practice in social science. He brings history and its complexity back in, and he does so in a clear and empirically informed way. For this reason, Inguscio's analysis sheds a light on the study of conflict and violence in Medieval Europe without the intellectual arrogance to try to demonstrate a de-contextualised theory.

Inguscio's approach refuses the dialectic that prescribes the turning out of a set of historical steps (according to a theoretical model developed in a different context at a different point in time) to achieve a certain aim. Inguscio's work powerfully reminds us that: 'the end of history' cannot be found, the reality of the European continent and Medieval Genoa is too pervaded by contradictory turning points to give confirmation of the fact that social scientists are absolutely right. In spite of the work of Putnam, Fukuyama, and Greif, history is endless and a rich source of surprises (Tollebeek 1998: 353).

Emanuele Ferragina
*Assistant Professor of Sociology
at Sciences Po Paris*, and
*Associate Member of the
Department of Social Policy and Intervention,
University of Oxford*

Oxford
November, 2014

Foreword

References

Fukuyama, F. (1992) *The End of History and the Last Man*. London: Penguin.

Putnam, R. D. (1993) *Making Democracy Work: Civic Traditions in Modern Italy*. Princeton, NJ: Princeton University Press.

Tollebeek, J. (1998) 'Historical Representation and the Nation-State in Romantic Belgium', *Journal of the History of Ideas*, 59, 329–353.

Preface

I am writing this introduction after a short visit to the Archivio di Stato in Genoa. After discussing with local experts the current state of affairs of the Genoese historical literature, I am reinforced in my conviction of the importance of publishing this research in the format of its original submission of 2008. Since then, I have changed my mind on many of the larger implications of the events described in this book, but I have yet to discover anything that disproves the validity of the conclusions reached here or makes it obsolete. The conflict dimension of the history of Genoa still needs to be properly disclosed if we are to better our understanding of the social, political and economic development of one of the most important cities of medieval Europe.

Since completing this research I have expanded it greatly through my doctoral and postdoctoral studies at Oxford and Yale. As a consequence almost nothing of the 2008 manuscript, my dissertation for the M.Sc. degree from Oxford on which this monograph is based, found its way in its original form into my other current projects. As it stands, this book is for me both an important contribution to the state of the literature and the beginning of an intellectual journey seeking to uncover the role played by civil conflict to the economic and political development of Genoa.

The historical issue that I address in this study is the civil strife among Genoese families in the twelfth century. The history of Genoa is extremely well documented compared to other cities in the same period. Thus it is possible to build an effective factual account of the phenomenon of conflict. Moreover, the availability of the *Notarili* allows the economic dimension of civil conflicts to be properly displayed. By this I mean that I will enquire into the economics of the conflict. This will include: the effects of civil conflicts on the economic connections between families and the financial, human and social capital invested in a confrontation. The costs of war and the costs of peace must be taken into account if we are to construct a complex social and economic analysis of conflict.

AGOSTINO INGUSCIO

Cape Town
April, 2014

ACKNOWLEDGEMENTS

This book was written in England, while I attended the University of Oxford to study for a Master of Science in Economic and Social History. Its first draft – in the form of my Master's dissertation - was awarded the Charles Feinstein Prize for the Best Graduate Dissertation in Economic and Social History.

My thanks go in particular to Professor Andrea Zorzi and Andrea Zerbini for encouraging me to go to Oxford, and to Professor Chris Wickham for directing me, some years ago, to commence the postgraduate research which led to this book.

My grateful acknowledgements are due to the University of Oxford and the economic and social history group. Furthermore I wish to thank the Regione Toscana for providing initial support for my graduate studies.

St. John's College provided the perfect setting in which to complete this work. The friends that I met at St John's were essential in providing help and support while writing this book. In particular I am thankful to my friends Jon Day and Patrick Lantschner for all their support. Without Jon, it would not have been possible to complete this work.

I have learned a great deal from my fellow students, with whom I have discussed many of the themes treated here. In particular I am thankful for the advice and friendship of Tobias Pforr, Andrei Pesic, Jeremy Schneider, Ferdinando Giugliano, Emanuele Ferragina, Alberto Rigolio, Stephanie Brockerhoff, Danielle Connolly and Hanaan Marwah.

I thank all of them and the many others who made my first year at the University of Oxford one that I will always remember and cherish.

I dedicate this book to Franco Bassani and Italo Inguscio.

A.I.

REINTERPRETING GENOESE CIVIL CONFLICTS

INTRODUCTION

The historical issue that I will address in this monograph is the civil conflicts between the Genoese families in the years 1174-96 described by Ottobono the scribe in his *Annales* of the city. During the period in question, one of Genoa's main characteristics was the almost constant confrontations and clashes between different family factions.

The city's *Annales* allow us to construct a factual account of the phenomenon of conflict. The eminent Genoese historian, Vitale, remind us how hard it has been to conceptualize these violent actions: 'Every attempt of giving order to the chaos of clashes ... appears as a desperate endeavour'.[1]

Fundamental progress towards describing the phenomenon of Genoese civil conflict was made in the 1970s by scholars interested in the structure of families, groups or clans. These historians used anthropological, sociological and demographic methods, aimed not at reconstructing the *genetic* story of a family but to understand the dynamics, evolution and behaviour of these groups. This kind of approach, typical of the French *nouvelle histoire,* can be seen in the important works of Grendi, Heers and Hughes that focused on internal group relations in Genoa, particularly in the thirteenth, fourteenth and fifteenth centuries.[2] Even though such studies are very valuable, suggesting a fruitful new approach to the issue I have outlined above, they do have their limitations. Many of the *nouvelle histoire* historians somehow failed to place such groups in the socio-political dimension of the conflicts, and their research found itself divided into a number of individual

---

[1] Vitale, *Breviario*, p. 29. Full citations are found in the Bibliography.

[2] Grendi, *Profilo*; Heers, *Le clan*; Hughes, 'Urban growth', and *'Ideali domestici'*.

monographies, falling short of giving us a better understanding of the complex dynamics inside the city of Genoa.[3]

Heers grounded faction solidly in communal history but did it in a polemical way.[4] He dismissed the interpretations provided by scholars who had written on medieval politics as 'erroneous', 'puerile' and 'useless'.[5] In an attempt to attack the authors he labelled 'economic determinists', Heers concluded with a tautological explanation of events, saying that violent behaviour originated in the inherently violent context of the era.[6] Better academic value can be found in his works dedicated to the family structure in Genoan society.[7]

These are part of a historiography that tries to reconstruct the evolution of family behaviours themselves. This approach can be found in works by such scholars as Grendi and Hughes whose works are an important background for any scholar endeavouring to explore the civil conflicts in Genoa. Through the study of dowries, wills, filial emancipation, inheritance and geographical position of the households, these scholars allow us to understand the characters and ideals of the principal actors responsible for the civil unrest in Genoa.[8]

The Genoese families and their individual members are going to be the central characters of this work, so I shall briefly outline the main characteristics of these social groups. The family structures that emerge from the sources are strongly vertical and patrilineal; characterized by the repetition of the same names generation after generation, and by the utilization of the same surname starting from the twelfth century. The

---

[3] Petti Balbi, 'Strutture Familiari', pp. 17-18.

[4] Zorzi, 'La cultura', p. 16.

[5] Heers, *Le clan*, p. 16, cf. Molho, 'Review', p. 134.

[6] An additional weakness is outlined in Dean, 'Marriage and Mutilation', p. 7. The author underlines how Heers draws heavily on Florentine examples and laws to sustain his generalization.

[7] Heers, *Le livre des comptes*.

[8] Grendi, *Profilo*, and Hughes, 'Urban growth'.

Introduction

family possessions passed to sons or to brothers. Common economic interests between fathers and adult sons were maintained. The head of the family lived in the *domus magna* in the city and controlled an adjoining tower, which was always inherited by one of his sons – normally the eldest.[9] The central importance of these lineage groups is also shown in the marriages between its members. These were contracted by the heads of the households, usually to strengthen the ties with families they were already allied with.[10]

Hughes argued that the Genoese families 'behaved as a hierarchical unit'.[11] In the majority of cases it is therefore hard to argue that civil conflicts broke out because of the obligation of kinsmen to react to an injury, and that *vendetta* was fed by a sense of harmonious correspondence between crime and expiation.[12] Dean showed that civil conflict was not the automatic, irrational response of a kin group in the face of injury or threat, but a rationalised, perhaps economically motivated, stratagem. As he points out: 'Kin could choose the vendettas they wished to pursue'.[13] Zorzi has also argued that initiating a confrontation between factions was often far from irrational, and could come about after long tactical planning.[14] Indeed, in our period the vendetta operated by the family of a killed member against his murderer rarely happened. Yet however valuable, these analyses often failed to consider how and why these families interacted with each other, and the issue of conflict among them is somehow avoided. In Hughes' words, the conflicts were all too often 'seemingly pointless'.[15]

---

[9] Hughes, 'Urban growth', p. 10.

[10] On the structure of Genoese families see Hughes, 'Urban growth', pp. 13-16.

[11] Hughes, 'Urban growth', p. 66.

[12] Heers, *Le clan*, p. 118.

[13] Dean, 'Marriage and Vendetta', p. 21.

[14] Zorzi, 'La cultura', p. 139.

[15] Hughes,'Urban growth', p. 7.

The fact that the historiography has too often undervalued or misrepresented the analysis of these conflicts consistently undermines our understanding of this communal society. Indeed if we are asked to find a trait common to the very different urban societies of communal Italy, it could well be the conflict-based nature of the social relations within them.[16] Clearly, the time is ripe for taking our understanding of the conflicts occurring within Genoese society to a deeper level. Recent writings – those of Zorzi in particular – have recognised the fundamental political importance of civil struggles within such societies.[17] I intend to shed more light on the structure of these conflicts from this standpoint.

Roberts warned us to 'not let the arguments be coloured by our own values and preconceptions' and not to look at conflicts exclusively 'in terms of failure'.[18] Indeed I argue that Genoese society was permeated by conflict, and that civil confrontations were indeed one of the conceivable bargaining means for conducting political debate. Thus they were always present – at least in a latent state – in the communal life even when the *Annales* did not report any violent events happening in the city. I will show this by outlining that within certain limits violence was accepted and by showing the strong correlation between alliance in the civil conflicts and commercial and trust ties. This shows that the conflict inherent in the political life of the city was not something derived from particular events, but was in fact a constant feature of Genoese society. In what follows I will show that the various economic activities of the Genoese citizens were organized precisely so that they would not be overly disrupted by internal conflicts. Indeed when there were commercial ties between families, they operated as retardants of the conflict's escalation.

---

[16] Zorzi, 'La cultura', p. 138.

[17] Zorzi, 'La cultura', p. 137.

[18] Roberts, *Order and Dispute*, p. 167.

Introduction

Such an analysis is perfectly aligned with the renewed attempts by economic historians to define interpretative schemes of civil conflicts, and it will allow me to develop a constructive critique of the work of Greif. In his new book, he has proposed an interpretation of the economic and social dimensions of conflicts among Genoese factions during the period under consideration.[19] My findings differ from his. In my view, his interpretation of the events that lead to the transition from a consular system to the election of one *podestà* is poorly sustained by the sources available. Aware of these possible risks, I will utilise the documents to present and elucidate my position regarding this institutional evolution and what we might call the 'economy of conflict'. As already mentioned, I will explore the ways in which the economic actors of Genoa prevented their commercial transactions from being severely damaged when a conflict exploded in the city. Furthermore I will show evidence of the capital – monetary and non – invested by the families involved in civil conflicts. These range from real estate transactions in order to reinforce the defences of a family, to utilising the specific fighting skills acquired overseas by some families, to the heavy investments in social capital – through the foundation of a church – in order to reacquire legitimacy lost because of the aggressive actions committed.

---

[19] Greif, *Institutions*.

1

SOURCES UTILISED

The first challenge for the historian who wants to explore the complex dynamics of communal society in the twelfth century is the scarcity of the sources that survive until the present. Any interpretation of the events should be solidly grounded on the historical evidence available. I will start this research from these sources.

The twelfth century for Genoa is extremely well documented compared to other cities in the same period. The fact that Communal society was essentially shaped by the practices of civil conflict is reflected by the structure of the sources. Indeed, our whole documentation is permeated by references to these conflicts. This is obvious for the Genoese chronicles, but it is also present in the sources produced by the public powers – statutes, council decisions, judicial and fiscal acts – and mercantile sources.

My starting point will be the *Annales*, begun in 1099 by the eminent citizen Caffaro. They are the oldest continuous exposition of the history of the city.[20] These memories, read to the consuls in 1152, received official status and were continued in an institutionalised context until 1293. Thus they are the only examples of an uninterrupted account continued for over two centuries and written by contemporaries. In these two cen-

---

[20] For this monograph I have used the most recent edition of the *Annales Ianuenses, Annales Genovesi di Caffaro e de' suoi continuatori* (hereinafter referenced as *Annales*).

turies, six further authors compiled them: Oberto Cancelliere, Ottobono the scribe, Ogerio Pane, Marchisio the scribe and Iacopo Doria. Later, in the period 1225-1293, the annals were compiled anonymously or by a collective of four eminent people chosen by the Commune officers. They provide an immensely valuable representation of the events of the city from day to day. As such, it is possible to use them to build a hugely effective factual account of the phenomenon of conflict in the city. For this book, civil conflict is considered as any reference in the *Annales* to dissensions, battles, wars, enmities, hatreds, homicides, etc. The chronicle for the period under consideration was composed by a public officer, the commune scribe Ottobono.[21] As such, this source is more an official documentary expression of the city government than a literary work. As has become clear, the *Annales* represent much more than the feelings of a single author. Because of their public dimension they can be taken as an expression of the views of the Genoan political élite on the events that characterized the history of the city. Considering the official role of the *Annales* of the city, a textual analysis of the narrative can outline the aspects of the ideological construction of conflict and it is an important testimony of the way in which the contemporaries perceived political conflict.

The first aspect that must be considered regards which point of view he was representing. This is a question that can be answered with an analysis of when the *Annales* were written, and under which authority. There is much evidence that would postpone the composition of the *Annales* until after the Sicilian expedition of 1194. In the *proemio*, the author informs us that his intention is to restart the work that had been interrupted for a long after Oberto Cancelliere had interrupted is work in 1173. Moreover Ottobono refers to the death of the emperor Frederick I in 1189. Yet, it is known that this event did not take

---

[21] Petti Balbi, *Una città*, pp. 252-255.

Sources

place until 1190.[22] Also, already in 1191, when mentioning the promises made by the Emperor Henry VI to obtain the Genoese cooperation to the conquest of Sicily, he called them lies and falsities.[23] Furthermore, during the description of the 1191 and of the 1194 Sicilian expeditions, the author mentions that Genoa was going to be deprived of its gains by the Emperor. These examples suggest that the author was well aware of events in advance, and was writing with the advantages of hindsight. However it must be remembered that Ottobono might well have taken some contemporary notes of the principal events as would be suggested by the details in the narrative after 1190. We can conclude, overall, that the final composition of the *Annales* of Ottobono (that is, when they were read in the city council and deposited in the commune's archive), began in that period of relative quiet and administrative reorganization that followed the civil wars. Probably in 1195 and 1196 under the *podestà* Giacomo Manerio and Drudo Marcellino.[24] This aspect is essential in order to understand the position of the author, and of the Commune, regarding the civil disputes.[25] Indeed rather than writing for future generations (or historians), Ottobono wrote primarily for the authorities whose consent he needed to preserve. In light of this, it is understandable that Ottobono constantly defends the consular activities and praises the *podestà*, who had probably given him the task of compiling the *Annales*.

This aspect makes it even more essential to use Ottobono's narrative alongside other sources, giving his work a contextual interpretation. I will also rely on the *Codice Diplomatico*, the work in which Imperiale collected and edited the various documents preserved in the Genoese archives, or transcribed in the

---

[22] *Annales*, p. 30.
[23] *Annales*, p. 36.
[24] *Annales*, p. 60.
[25] *Annales*, p. XXI.

commune's own *Libri Iurium*. These integrate the chronicles with references to political life, foreign policy, and military activities of the city. The 598 documents cover the period between the origins of the commune in 1099 and 1200. An analysis of these documents shows that the foreign policy of the city was of high profile, even if this is sometimes not mentioned in the *Annales*, and does not seem to suffer particularly from the city's internal divisions.[26]

In order to interpret the conflicts mentioned in the *Annales*. I relied on commercial documents. Italian notary documents appeared for the first time after 1150 in Genoa, and nowhere else before 1200, so from this point of view too, its twelfth-century sources are unmatched.[27] The Genoese notarial contracts are a more important source of information on this subject than has hitherto been realised.[28] These documents, for the economic historian, are priceless, but they have never been used extensively to analyse the dramatic aspects of the city's political life.[29] Indeed they seem, in the words of Vitale, 'to ignore the conflicts'.[30] It is true that other historians, most importantly Hughes, do use these sources for information on family structures. However, regarding the phenomenon of civil conflict, Hughes merely concludes that they are useless for such a study.[31]

The documents that we will consider are complete business documents, the contents of which were enforceable in courts of law. The people involved in these contracts (and their witnesses), would agree on a deal in front of the notary who would

---

[26] 'Avvertenza' in *Codice*, pp. XII-XV.

[27] McGovern, 'The Documentary', p. 227.

[28] On the editions of the twelfth century Genoese documents see also: Moresco and Bagnetti, *L'edizione dei notai liguri*.

[29] Abulafia, *The Two Italies*, p. 60.

[30] Vitale, *Breviario*, p. 29.

[31] Hughes, 'Urban Growth', p. 7.

Sources

then write an *imbreviatura*, a summary of the actual contract, in his book, or *cartulare*. This summary usually reported the date of the registration in front of the notary, the place in which it was registered, the people involved and the details of the commercial agreements, real estate transactions, marriage contracts or wills that were registered.

The *Notarile* of Oberto for the year 1186 is composed of 346 acts dated from September 22, 1186 to December 24 of the same year.[32] For the year 1190, we have 680 documents surviving. The first *imbreviatura* was written on January 11, 1190 and the last on August 23, though there are plenty of voids between the two dates.[33]

A more complete cartulary is the one of Guglielmo Cassinese. This contains consecutive acts dated from December 26, 1190, to April 26, 1192; there are 1900 acts in total. None of the early notarial records are complete for as long a period as the Cassinese register. None of the other notaries whose acts are extant for the same period drew up as many acts as Cassinese, or as many commercial documents, affairs of navigation, and civil acts.[34] His clientele was largely made of leading Genoese families, who will be discussed later.[35]

Documents similar to those contained in the *Notarili* are the ones regarding the economic activities of the Monastery of San Siro. Most of these documents are edited in the collection *Le Carte* containing 71 documents for the period 1160-1200. The documents are of various kinds: the cartulary contains real estate transactions, juridical sentences, papal letters, elections of abbeys, absolutions, excommunications, wills etc. The monastery of San Siro did not have a dedicated notary, but it used different notaries from the city. This is reflected in the

---

[32] *Oberto Scriba da Mercato 1186* (hereinafter referenced as *Oberto 1186*).

[33] *Oberto Scriba de Mercato, 1190* (hereinafter referenced as *Oberto 1190*).

[34] De Roover, 'The Business Records', p. 43.

[35] On *Cassinese* see also Schwarz, 'Two Sources'.

documents, which are similar from every point of view to the documents contained in the *Notarili*, except that they more regularly concern real estate issues.[36] The connections outlined by the contracts are of two different kinds. Some families had strong interests in common, that is the case when two families registered many contracts describing joint operations; others had limited 'connections of trust', that is two families were confident in registering their contracts in presence of political allies but did not invest in common operations.[37] Furthermore I used the evidence of commercial relations between families involved in civil conflicts to divide these events into two types. Some were indeed caused by unidentifiable factors happening between families who were not political opponents and did not last for long. The information contained in the notary documents show that the conflicts that were resolved had as protagonist individuals who shared economic interests that acted as peace keeping elements.

The majority, however, were manifestations of the political struggle between two main factions that can be clearly identified using the *Notarili*; those confrontations tended to last much longer and to reemerge in later years with different protagonists. I identify the two factions as the de Volta faction and the de Curia faction. de Volta/de Frexia, Scoto, de Castello, de Mari, Spinola and Grimaldo were the families linked to the first faction; and de Curia, Porcello, Lecaleio, Bulbunoso, Pevere, de Turca and Avvocato were members of the second.[38] This interpretation resolved one puzzle left unresolved from the reading of the *Annales*, namely why several conflicts seem to

---

[36] See 'Introduzione' in *Le Carte*.

[37] This risk is stated openly in one document of the San Siro collection. *Le Carte*, doc. 139. Granovetter, 'The Strength of Weak Ties', calls this 'mutual confiding', p. 1361.

[38] De Volta and de Frexia were effectively the same families; Olivieri, 'Cronologia', pp. 199, 209, 213, states that Ingo de Frexia was the son of Ingone de Volta.

Sources

have been successfully resolved, while others continued until the final showdown of the years 1192-1194.

In order to demonstrate this, I will track the relations of these families at every level: their members can appear as economic actors, guarantors, councillors, family of the protagonists of a transaction, and witnesses; or they might just have hosted the scribe and the parties involved in registering the contract in their house or shop. Genoese communal society emerged as one dominated by civil conflicts. The *Notarili* representing the commercial life in Genoa at the height of conflict could not be immune to it; indeed, as we shall see, they are imbued by it.[39] Clearly, it is the correlation between the actors involved in civil conflicts and the economic actors of the *Notarili* that we are looking for in order to strengthen our understanding of the period. Also what is not found in the *Notarili* is significant for our task. I believe it to be telling that, after analysing more than two thousand documents in which the names of our characters figure constantly, in almost none of them do the names of two people that were represented as adversaries in the *Annales* – directly or as members of a faction – appear together, either as commercial partners or as witnesses. This shows how an economic relationship between two parties reflected at least political neutrality, thus confirming the relevance of the commercial documents for our analysis. The few exceptions to this rule underline the utility of an *Annales-Notarili* comparison.

Because of the disproportion between the length of each year in Ottobono's narration, the period 1174-1189 and the period 1190-1196 are roughly equal. Moreover the second period is characterized by an evolution of communal institutions and of the civil conflict characteristics. Thus I divided my analysis in two chapters regarding the different periods.[40]

---

[39] Zorzi, 'La Cultura', p. 138.

[40] *Annales*, pp. 3-33 and pp. 34-66.

2

A Crescendo Ground Noise of Conflicts, 1174-1189

In 1174-1177, the author makes no mention of the issue of political unrest in the city. Indeed, for the year 1177 it is said that the city was living 'in peace and fertility'.[41] From the beginning of 1178, however, Ottobono began to mention rising levels of tension within the city. In this year, the Mazanello and the Navarro families fought once, but by the end 'peace' and 'concord', between the antagonists were restored.[42] In 1179, following the death of one of the consuls, Baldizio Usumari (of natural causes) two important families, the Vento and the Grillo, whose members were consuls in the same year, fought.[43] The author mentioned the beginning of 'dissension' between them that flew into a battle in the valley of Sturla, outside the city. However, already in 1180 the confrontation seemed resolved, and indeed the author wrote that the two families 'made peace and concord'.[44] In these first descriptions of civil tensions, Ottobono used the dichotomy 'concord' and 'dissension'. Indeed in both occasions the adversaries fought violently against each other. However the author stated also that those hostilities did not last for long. As an initial comment

---

[41] *Annales*, p. 11.
[42] *Annales*, p. 12.
[43] *Annales*, p. 14.
[44] *Annales*, p. 12.

on the terminology used by the author, I should stress that the phenomenon of conflicts between Genoese families was not depicted dramatically. Furthermore, it is evident that the role of the commune's officers was not to prevent the conflicts; they were called merely to compose the conflicts and to reach an agreement between the parties, so as to avoid escalations. There were no negative comments or accusations by the author, just a description of the events as they occurred. Clearly, therefore, tensions inside the city walls were not uncommon and were not perceived as a menace to the survival of the commune. Moreover these first conflicts were not depicted in any illustrations. We should stress again that when Ottobono was writing he had already seen the consequences of the various events, so perhaps we may consider the lightness of his terminology as dependent on the lack of consequences of these two first conflicts. This is a very important aspect, because it would tell us that the civil conflict in itself was not condemned by the commune; what was condemned were the eventual consequences of these conflicts. I will show a much stronger moral condemnation for the other conflicts under consideration. This depended not on their different initial characteristics, but on their much more dangerous effects on the commune's life.

The question regarding these first two events is then clearly why the action of the consuls in these cases was arguably successful, in that the Mazanello and Navarro families are never again mentioned in the *Annales* in relation to violent actions. The author did not give any information that could help us understand this. Thus, we must rely on the commercial documents. In the *Notarile* of Oberto, the family names Mazanello and Navarro appear twice, and once in the *Notarile* of Guglielmo: significantly they always compare on the same documents as partners. From these we learn that on March 31, 1190 Mazanello and Navarro declared that they owed 120 Lire to the merchant Gandolfo from Piacenza. On August 14, 1190 the same two declared that they owed 72 Lire to the merchant

Ground Noise of Conflicts

Gillano from Piacenza and on July 8, 1191 they committed themselves to pay back a 51 lire debt they contracted together.[45] In the first two documents Oberto states that the debts had been contracted to buy commercial goods; for the third one the deadline, typical for trade loans, fixed on August 1, makes us believe that the money was borrowed for a mercantile enterprise.[46] This is relevant because a commercial partnership in the period was a delicate and risky business, especially if the amount invested was significant.[47] It required a high level of trust between the partners and was unlikely to be made with a political adversary.

From these documents I concluded that the 'dissensions' which happened in 1178 between the Mazanello and the Navarro had been resolved permanently. Moreover, I propose that economic ties between the families were probably already present in 1178, and they helped to stop the confrontation at the beginning. This suggests that the 1178 battle can be disconnected from the chain of murderous events that followed that. Furthermore the names of Navarro or Mazanello do not appear linked, even tenuously (as witnesses for example), with names we are going to be familiar with as involved in conflicts.

The events of 1179 are recalled by Hughes and described as 'a minor skirmish', one of the constant confrontations between families.[48] However the simple collocation of this event as part of the confrontation between the two different factions that were defining themselves in those years in Genoa is not satisfactory. Indeed, after this battle, a permanent truce was reached. In the *Notarile* of Oberto Scriba, the Vento and Grillo

---

[45] *Oberto 1190*, docs. 312, 629; *Cassinese*, doc. 813.

[46] For the dates characteristic of a sea loan, see Hoover, 'The Sea Loan', p. 503.

[47] Casaretto, 'La moneta genovese', pp. 180-188. The value of Genoese lira at the end of the twelfth century is widely accepted to be 8,6 grams of gold. 1 lira was divided in 20 soldi. 1 soldo was divided in 12 denari.

[48] Hughes, 'Urban growth', p. 8.

families figure together in a document in which Pietro Vento declares that a Grillo completed his payment for buying a house.[49] They also left many records of their economic activities in the *Notarile* of Guglielmo Cassinese in 1191 and 1192. It is very significant to note that in 17% – a high percentage – of the documents containing the name Grillo, it appears jointly with the name Vento.[50] Clearly the families, at least between 1186 and 1192, were not enemies, and did not fear an attack from each other, considering especially how the majority of these transactions were written in the house of the Vento. It is hard to believe that in a moment of such extreme violence, somebody was willing to go into the house of an adversary for business reasons. I would conclude that the 1179 events were truly a minor skirmish, as noted by Hughes. However they were not part of the main hostilities. The two parties were economically connected, and were only briefly adversaries at the time of the death of Baldizio Usumari, probably as a consequence of the failure in reaching an agreement as to how to fill up the power vacuum that followed this event. Their common interests once again stopped the hostilities at their inception.[51]

From 1180 we start to perceive some differences in the perception that the author had of the civil conflicts he reported, reflected in a noticeable evolution of style. Ottobono wrote that 'a great hatred and war' grew between Rubaldo Porcello and his brothers, and Girardo Scoto and his family.[52] The author stated that the consuls mediated to restore the peace between these two eminent members of Genoese élite but he informed us also that Girardo refused the peace and left Genoa. At that point the consuls ordered all his properties to be destroyed. Ottobono

---

[49] *Oberto 1186*, doc. 230.

[50] These are 11 documents out of 63 in total for the Grillo family. *Cassinese*, docs. 86, 106, 269, 495, 523, 527, 634, 1056, 1205, 1331, 1816.

[51] Notice that the Grillo family is present in both Vento's network representations, pp. 51, 52.

[52] *Annales*, p. 15.

Ground Noise of Conflicts

was aware of the special importance of this event compared to the previous occurrences of 'disagreement'. The author now spoke of a 'great hatred': not of a momentary 'disagreement', then, but of something more continuous and deep. It is essential again to consider that Ottobono was writing when this event had already demonstrated its destructive capabilities. Otherwise the evolution of his language would not make sense, as it referred to a contrast that had not escalated into a proper battle yet.

Why did the conciliatory mission of the consuls fail at this time? Firstly the *Annales* reported that Rubaldo in the same year was an important officer of the commune. I start to perceive that the control of public offices was part of the confrontation although Ottobono frequently stated the consuls' fairness and good governance. Moreover, given the patterns visible in the last two examples we have looked at, it is crucial to note that from the *Notarili* we can see that the two families never had any economic connections. I am here dealing with hostility between two powerful families, probably traditionally adversaries, and unmediated by any economic links. Porcello, as a 'consul for justice', perhaps had the possibility of forcing on the Scoto party what seemed to them an unfair agreement, which was thus refused. With the authorities backing his opponent, Scoto preferred to escape from the city. The consequences of this unsolved dispute for the city were going to last. From this time on I will show that all the numerous events recounted in the *Annales* were not irrational and pointless, but can be interpreted (with the help of the *Notarili*) as a single war. However, it is important to notice that these two families were not going to face each other directly again in the narration. This is because the dynamics of Genoese civil conflicts were strictly political. Thus, they not followed the vendetta pattern described by Dean.[53] There was no necessity for each particular family to gain revenge against a direct target. The struggle was

---

[53] Dean, 'Marriage and Vendetta', p. 21.

carried on year by year by different individuals, that were, as we shall demonstrate, members of defined and separate factions. From now on I will state the membership of the de Volta or de Curia factions of every family involved in the violent actions. Most of the time – I will state when this is not the case – the *Annales* do not help us in this task, but we can achieve this utilising the commercial records.

The Scoto were members of the de Volta faction. This is demonstrated by a number of documents that connect the family with the de Castello, de Frexia and de Volta.[54] Particularly interesting is a document relating to a real estate transaction. In 1191, the sons of Girardo Scoto sell a house with the permission of Opizone de Castello and Adalasia, daughter of Girardo, refers to Guglielmo and Opizone de Castello, sons of Opizone de Castello, as her family.[55] In the same year, Ogerio Scoto completes the transaction of real estate 'with the suggestion and under the authority' of his uncle Guglielmo de Castello.[56] This document shows further the close family relationship between the Scoto and the de Castello. Furthermore, when Adalasia Scoto registered her will, the witnesses included two members of the de Castello family.[57]

One document of 1192 locates a Porcello in the house of Ogerio Vento. I will show the closeness of the Vento family to the de Curia faction in that year.[58]

In 1181 and 1182, Ottobono does not mention any events of internal conflict. However it is significant to note the total absence of mentions of 'peace' etc. This evident stylistic difference in comparison to the previous years is probably due to the rising tension in the city. Knowing what happened in the following years the peaceful biennium can well be defined as

---

[54] *Cassinese*, for de Frexia, docs. 385, 60; for de Volta, doc.1426.

[55] *Cassinese*, doc. 61.

[56] *Cassinese*, doc. 692.

[57] *Cassinese*, doc. 658.

[58] *Cassinese*, doc. 1538.

Ground Noise of Conflicts

preparation for the incoming tempest. The reactions to the events of 1180 could have been delayed by a strong plague that hit the city killing many nobles.[59]

Focal is the fact that Genoa restarted its war with Pisa in 1182.[60] This and other external wars were fought by Genoa even in the years characterized by the worst civil hostilities. It is important to outline this fact because it confirms the findings of Otterbein: that in societies characterized by the presence of fraternal interest groups 'war and feuding go hand-in-hand'.[61]

Civil conflicts got back on stage in 1183, which Ottobono described as a year whose principal characteristics were the explosions of violence between fellow citizens. In this year, 'many hatreds and divisions were in the city'.[62] The protagonists were Folcone de Castello, supported by the Vento family, and his adversaries Bulbunoso and 'those de Curia'. The Annalist spoke of a 'great war' fought by the two groups in the valley of Bisanne. The importance of this event is further stressed by an illustration, the first one representing a civil conflict.[63] It represents two fully armoured knights charging against each other. The picture outlines the fact that these clashes were often organized by the fighters. Indeed this was probably the case in the already mentioned battle between Grillo and Vento in 1179. In both cases the contenders met out of the city fully prepared for a clash and fought.[64] This shows the presence of a custom that appears to exacerbate the conflicts in Genoa. Indeed, the miniature is very impressive recalling external war representations, but in doing so restrained 'the conflicts form

---

[59] *Annales*, p. 16.

[60] *Annales*, p. 17.

[61] Otterbein, 'Internal War', p. 1479.

[62] *Annales*, p. 19.

[63] *Annales*, Tav. II, fig. XV; all the illustrations relevant for this text have been included in the Appendix, below, pp. 81-88.

[64] On the preparations required for this sort of confrontation see Maire Vigueur, *Cittadini e Cavalieri*.

destroying the wider social order'.[65] That is why even in a year characterized by explosions of internal violence the author stated that the consuls arrived at the end of their mandate with honour and maintained the *iuris ordo* – rule of law – in the city.[66]

The de Castello were part of the faction de Volta. The de Castello and the de Volta also had family links. For instance from a document of March 31, 1191 we find out that Bellobruno de Castello sold to the Abbey of San Quirico the land that he has received from Rosso de Volta as a dowry for her daughter.[67] Also the Scoto family was a member of the de Volta coalition. We have seen one of its members fighting two years earlier against Porcello, a member, along with Bulbunoso, of the faction known as de Curia. I have located Bulbunoso in the de Curia faction, because he is mentioned fighting alongside them on the two occasions, in 1183 as we have just noted, and again in 1194. The name Bulbunoso is mentioned twice in the *Notarile* of Cassinese. The documents report that he bought a land in Genoa from Ogerio Vento in 1191.[68] In that year the Vento family was connected to the de Curia. Moreover it is possible to find another external confirmation to my hypothesis. A document dated December 17, 1175, right at the beginning of the period considered in this dissertation, reports a donation of a land to the monastery of San Siro.[69] The donors are listed as Bulbunoso and his brother Angeleto. For this operation his witnesses were Lanfranco and Guglielmo Pevere, whom I will locate in the de Curia faction thanks to information contained both in the *Annales* and in the *Notarili*. Furthermore,

---

[65] Gluckman, 'The Peace', p.1.

[66] *Annales*, p. 20.

[67] *Cassinese*, docs. 399, 400.

[68] *Cassinese*, docs. 1412, 1413.

[69] Authentic copy of the 1656, in *Archivio Durazzo Giustiniani*, Genealogie I\7.5, c. 1 (originally in 'Actis Guglielmi Caligepalii notarii in Sancto Syro').

Ground Noise of Conflicts

Bulbunoso appears as one of the witnesses in the will of Giacomo de Turca registered on August 6, 1205.[70] Similarly, in an appendix to the same document Giacomo declares that Adele, the daughter of Bulbunoso, lent him money on different occasions.[71] As I shall show, the adherence to the de Curia faction of the de Turca family is widely demonstrated.

The Vento in this period were close to the de Volta faction, but I will outline their progressive separation from this coalition in the *Notarili*. From a document of 1190 we see that Pietro Vento was married to Maria, daughter of Ottone de Castello.[72] I have already stated that numerous documents show the high level of trust between the Vento and the de Volta coalition members in that period. However one of these shows well one peculiarity of their partnerships. On September 24, 1186 Fulco son of Fulco de Castello, accepted in *accomendacio* – a type of loan – from Rufo de Volta 307 lire for commerce in Constantinople. 41 of these Lire were lent by Simone Vento, and witnesses were Simone and Tommaso Vento. Oberto Scriba registered this contract in the house of Bonifacio de Volta.[73] All the documents involving Vento and de Volta members suggest that these two families in 1186 were indeed allied, most of the Vento documents were registered in the house of a de Volta member. The documents also show that Vento members acted as witnesses for de Volta ones and vice versa. However their economic ties were not strong. The only transaction in which a Vento invested his money in an operation involving a de Volta was the one already mentioned, significantly at the benefit of a de Castello, a family member then. From the documents we can certainly state that Vento members felt safe in the de Volta proprieties, but that their economic ties were not particularly strong.

---

[70] *Le Carte*, doc. 164.

[71] *Le Carte*, doc. 165.

[72] *Oberto 1190*, doc. 276.

[73] *Oberto 1186*, doc. 26.

During the following year the attention of Ottobono is captured by the aggression of 'those of Porto Maurizio', a small port town close to Genoa, and of 'an assembly of rebels' against the city.[74] Genoa often had to struggle to maintain its control over the smaller cities of the *riviere* (the coasts lying on both sides of Genoa). On this occasion it is evident that people that had to leave the city as a consequence of the civil conflicts of 1180 and 1183 joined forces with the people of Porto Maurizio to return. The author describes attentively the preparations for defence made by the consuls. However, before the confrontation the officers and the 'elders' of the rebels went to Genoa to 'kneel to the consuls'.[75] Ottobono here outlined the importance of this event with an illustration; the rebels are represented on their knees imploring the consuls for forgiveness.[76] However Ottobono affirmed that they surrendered before the fight even started. Probably the reality was that the rebels managed to be reaccepted in the city again. Stylistically the use of the term 'rebel' shows how Ottobono perceived that a full-blown civil war had been avoided only by an agreement in extremis.

In 1185, the peace was maintained and the author stated that the 'consuls brought back peace in Genoa'.[77] The years 1185 and 1186 passed indeed without any mention of conflict. But it is clear that the 'great peace' and 'tranquillity' that characterized the city were covering up a conflict that was about to start again at an entirely new level, challenging the very integrity of the city.[78]

From 1187 the internal conflict of Genoa reached previously unseen levels. The language utilized by the author evolved again. The first few lines of the text are worth quoting to show

---

[74] *Annales*, p.19.

[75] *Annales*, p. 19.

[76] *Annales*, Tav. III, Fig. 16 (reproduced below, p. 82).

[77] *Annales*, p. 22.

[78] *Annales*, p. 22.

the ways in which this transition manifested itself: 'Satan lifted his head. Lanfranco, the son of Giacomo de Turca, possessed by a devil spirit, killed the consul Anglerio de Mari'.[79] The words of Ottobono had never previously been so strong. The reference to the intervention of the devil behind the crimes committed in the city is completely new in his text. Indeed the author knew that an agreement was not going to be reached before a full scale civil war had exploded. This religious and moral commentary became characteristic of Ottobono's literary style in the following years. From 1174 Ottobono had not mentioned the murders or the violent deaths of any specific citizen. Nor had the author ever felt the need to refer to the actual number of casualties. This was probably due to the fact that the deaths in civil conflicts before 1187 were never those of high social positions. Yet, at that time Lanfranco (the son of the 1187 consul Giacomo de Turca) killed the consul Anglerio de Mari, one of the most prominent public figures of the city. Anglerio had been consul several times before 1187 and the fact that his murderer was the son of another consul, and an important public figure himself, was extremely relevant. The author did not have any doubt when he wrote that 'this homicide would have caused infinite hatreds in Genoa'; presumably the author represented the point of view of the commune. A murder of such importance could not pass without consequences, and afterward a group of nobles and people of the city destroyed the tower and the proprieties of the de Turca family and forced the killer into exile.[80] These measures did not prevent the escalation of the conflict, however. In the same year, two other important members of the city elite were killed: Rubaldo Porcello and Opizo Lecaleio. The first had been consul in 1180, when he was the protagonist of a violent confrontation with Girardo Scoto (as we have seen), and also in 1184; the second was consul in

---

[79] *Annales*, p. 22.

[80] *Annales*, p. 22. This destruction is represented in an illustration in *Annales*, Tav. III, fig. 16 (reproduced below, p. 82).

1183. The importance of the double homicide is evident, but the author did not attempt to describe the possible reasons behind these crimes. This year was a very difficult one for the city, which was not only weakened by internal strife but also had to consider complicated external events, with Saladin reconquering Jerusalem and attacking Tyre, and the Pisans menacing the Genoese positions in Sardinia. It might be thought that so many external enemies might have helped the reestablishment of internal peace, but again this certainly did not occur. From the point of view of Ottobono's literary style, we must note the length of the description of the events in the Crusader kingdoms, and particularly the help that Genoa gave in defending Tyre. This is essential because in 1190 we will see how the author gave different relevance to the external events and was well aware of their importance for the internal dynamics of the city.

My hypothesis is that all these homicides were again part of the political struggle between the de Volta and de Curia factions. This is supported by the documents contained in the *Notarili* that collocate the de Turca family in the Curia faction and the de Mari in the de Volta one. The *Notarile* of Guglielmo Cassinese contains six documents involving Giacomo, the father of the killer.[81] In one of them we discover how, in 1191, Giovanni Avvocato sold, a house that was owned by Opizo Lecaleio to Mabilia Lecaleio, the mother of his wife Adalaxia. Giovanni did everything with the suggestions of his family Guglielmo Pevere and Giacomo de Turca. Clearly, Giovanni, who, as we shall see was to become consul of the Curia in 1194, was brother-in-law of Opizo Lecaleio, killed in 1187. Moreover he was a family member of the consul Lanfranco Pevere who had been killed in 1190, a year before this contract was registered, and of Giacomo de Turca, the father of the killer of the Anglerio de Mari.[82] Furthermore, we learn from another document that Pevere and

---

[81] *Cassinese*, docs. 253, 618, 796, 1729, 1784.

[82] *Cassinese*, doc. 253.

Ground Noise of Conflicts

de Turca, with Enrico Lecaleio, were counsellors and family of the above-mentioned widow of Opizo Lecaleio.[83]

In all the documents analyzed, the name of de Turca appears along with the names Avvocato, Lecaleio and Pevere. Moreover the great majority of those documents are registered in the house of the de Turca, an important detail considering that in 1191 it was presumably dangerous to spend time in houses of non-allied families. Thanks to this evidence, the de Turca family can undoubtedly be identified as one of the components of the de Curia faction.

I will now show the evidence that locates the de Mari in the de Volta faction. The de Mari family was not as much a protagonist of real estate transactions as the de Turca. As a consequence the documents collected in the commercial archives are not as clear. However the evidence is still substantial. The de Mari family appears in numerous documents, although their names are never in the same texts as the names of members of the de Curia coalition.[84] Moreover, the de Mari are connected to the de Castello, the de Volta and to the de Frexia, the main families of the de Volta coalition. Most importantly many documents were recorded in the houses of de Volta and de Frexia members. The same conclusions as have been reached for the de Turca family are valid (in the opposing faction), for the de Mari as well.[85]

The *Annales* do not report any reason for the killings of Porcello and Lecaleio, but, the *Notarili* demonstrate that they were both eminent members of the Curia party. Knowing this, we can conclude that the double homicide was a response to the killing of Anglerio de Mari. I have already shown which documents allow us to locate Opizo Lecaleio in the de Curia

---

[83] *Cassinese*, doc. 618.

[84] *Oberto 1186*, docs. 349, 206, 480; *Oberto 1190*, docs. 28, 125, 644, 658, 404, 244.

[85] *Cassinese*, docs. 1186, 1192, 1195, 1396.

faction. Even after his death he was recorded in numerous documents.[86]

In 1188, Ingone de Volta, an important officer of the commune and a leader of the de Volta faction, was hit on the head and killed 'by chance' – Ottobono wrote – by a stone while passing in front of the house of the sons of Malfante. In the same year, in June, Ugone de Volta, the archbishop of Genoa died of natural causes, an event that must have affected the family's influence. Bonifacio, archdeacon of San Lorenzo, was elected as archbishop.[87]

In 1189 Guglielmo Vento and the de Volta fought on the city streets. This is the only occasion in which Ottobono reported a change in the factions, but, as usual, he did not mention any reason behind this evolution. The Vento fought against the de Curia in 1183 and against the de Volta in 1189.[88]

The *Notarili* offer an extremely interesting testimony of the evolution of the relationship between the de Volta faction and the Vento family. We have already mentioned that in 1186 the Vento members registered almost all their transactions in the de Volta house. Indeed 9 documents, out of 12 containing the name Vento, report the names Vento and de Volta together.[89] In 1190 these *joint contracts* with the de Volta faction constitute only 3 out of 15 documents; in these documents the name Vento appears simply as witnesses in contracts involving a de Castello.[90] In 1191, none of the 34 documents containing the name Vento are linked with the names of family. Exactly the

---

[86] *Oberto 1190*, doc. 271; *Cassinese*, docs. 47, 70, 94, 183, 202, 272, 284, 310, 673, 824, 877, 993, 996, 1068, 1296, 1276, 1295, 1380, 1630.

[87] The Archbishop Bonifacio did not belong to any of the fighting families. Olivieri, 'Cronologia', p. 213.

[88] *Annales*, pp. 19, 30.

[89] *Oberto 1186*, docs. 47, 99, 100, 101, 234, 237, 240, 242, 309.

[90] Individuals of the Vento family figure as witnesses in *Oberto 1190*, docs. 198, 337, 424.

Ground Noise of Conflicts

same happens for the 12 documents of 1192.[91] It is essential to notice that this dramatic decrease did not depend on a slower economic activity of the de Volta families, nor from their scarce presence on the *Notarile* of Guglielmo Cassinese. The de Volta appear on a relevant and relatively constant number of documents in all the mentioned years. For the same crucial years the San Siro documents report the growing connections of the Vento with families closer to the de Curia, in this case with the Pevere. On 13 May 1189 Guglielmo Pevere swears he will transport Bernardo de Valle, Guglielmo Sanito and Gerardo Clavel, along with their people and goods, on his ship to Barcelona. In case of default Pevere will pay 12,000 lire. This is a huge sum and Ogerio Vento and others declare that they are his 'guarantors'.[92] Considering the amount of the payment it is unlikely that Pevere and Vento were adversaries in this moment. This fact is confirmed by a second document. In October 1191 Guglielmo Pevere sells his share of three mills to the monastery of San Siro. He owned the mills jointly with his brother, his nephew and Gugliemo Vento. From this we can see that the relations between the Vento family and the Pevere were ongoing.[93] This evolution of the relations Vento – de Volta could surprise the reader considering the fact that Pietro Vento married a de Castello. Given the matrimonial mechanisms showed by Hughes and Airaldi, the role of a wife and of a wedding are closely linked with the role of the dowry and of the marriage. But once this 'matrimonial-patrimonial' operation was secured, the role of a wife was secondary and could have influenced political decisions only with difficulty.[94] The effects of marriage on feud was very different in Genoese society from the one outlined by Gluckman for the Nuer society in which

---

[91] See the social network graph of the Vento family.

[92] Original *Archivio Segreto* in *Archivio Storico di Genova*, n. 27137A\20. Registration code: Lisciardelli, note 134.

[93] *Le Carte*, doc. 141.

[94] Airaldi, *Genova e la Liguria*, p. 467.

'each man is led by his interest and compelled by custom, to seek to be on good terms with his wife's kin'.[95] In the battle of 1183, the Vento supported the de Castello, showing a closeness also demonstrated by the decision of marrying a de Castello; this emerges also in the commercial documents that show how Vento members were safe in de Volta houses. However the relationship between the two families was compromised already in 1189, or at least not strong enough to prevent a change in the alliance system. This event outlines a striking deeper role of 'weak' commercial ties as opposed to 'strong' families and trust ties.[96] This passage is extremely important in defining the characteristics of Genoese conflicts and I am going to give an overall interpretation of this passage in the fourth chapter.[97]

---

[95] Gluckman, 'The Peace', p. 7.

[96] On the distinction between weak and strong ties see Granovetter, 'The Strength of Weak Ties'.

[97] See pp. 25-27 above.

3

AN ESCALATION IN CIVIL CONFLICTS AND AN INSTITUTIONAL EVOLUTION

I will now discuss the final period covered by the *Annales*, going from 1190 to 1196. Thanks to commercial documents it is possible to reinterpret a series of events that can well be defined as the most important ones described here. In this section, I will correct some mistakes in the interpretation of the sources that seriously biased the understanding of the conflicts considered. This further stresses the necessity of this new analysis. I will also give my interpretation of the institutional shift that marked the apex of the conflicts.

In 1190 internal and external events evidently became correlated. The kings of France and England met in Genoa in order to reach an agreement for the transportation of their troops, on their way to the East in the Third Crusade.[98] Moreover, many Genoese pilgrims and soldiers left the city to help defend the Kingdom of Jerusalem. They were lead by Guido Spinula, consul of the Commune, who was accompanied by Nicola Embriaco, Fulco de Castello, Simone d'Oria, Baldovino Guercio, Rosso de Volta, Spezapreda and many others.[99] These are also the last mentions of the participation of Genoa citizens in the Crusade. The events of the following years were closely connected both to the expedition of the nobles

---

[98] Epstein, *Genoa*, p. 87.

[99] *Annales*, p. 33.

mentioned above and to the omission of any further information on their regard.

In the same year, Genoa's consuls elected for the first time a *podestà* to rule the city in 1191. The *podestà* was one, foreign, officer.[100] This institutional evolution has been considered a direct answer, of all the city notables, to the inability of the consular regime to prevent the internal strife in the city. Ottobono's text is at the basis of such an interpretation. He stated that the consuls of the city elected Manegoldo de Tetocio, from Brescia, as a *podestà* in order to prevent the civil conflicts which the desire of many for the consular position started in the city.[101]

The decision did not succeed in preventing further strife. In 1190, the victim was once again one of the consuls, Lanfranco Pevere, who also covered that role in 1183 and 1185. Lanfranco was killed during a communal council, by Fulco de Castello and Guglielmo de Castello, sons of Fulco de Castello, another consul and the leader of one of the most important families of the city. The language utilized by the author does not leave any doubt regarding his perception of the homicide, that it caused a deep 'pain' to the city and was committed without 'any causes'.[102] It is precisely the causes of the failure of this institutional reform to prevent conflicts that we must discover. I believe the election of the Manegoldo to be nothing more than a new element of the civil confrontations themselves. The consuls 'voted' while Guido Spinola, Folco di Castello, Rosso de Volta and others among the political leaders of the de Volta faction were fighting in front of the walls of Acre, and thus they were not able to attend as usual to the election of their successors. The desire of the consuls who remained in Genoa was to exclude the faction led by the nobles that had left the city from the governance of the city.

---

[100] For an analysis of this institution see Maire Vigueur, *I Podesta`*.

[101] *Annales*, p. 36; Vitale, *Il Comune*, p. 6; Epstein, *Genoa*, p. 88.

[102] *Annales*, p. 37.

Escalating Civil Conflicts

The murder of Lanfranco Pevere was clearly a reaction towards this move.

I have already discussed some of the elements that point to the adherence of the Pevere family to the de Curia coalition. Moreover a document indicates that the families Pevere, Avvocato, de Turca and Bulbunoso owned a property collectively. On March 24, 1192 Guglielmo Cassinese registered that Drua sold an *octena* – an eighth – of a property to the church of Santa Margherita of Murvallo. The other proprietors of the estate were Avvocato, Pevere, Giacomo de Turca and Bulbunoso.[103] A year before the attack of the de Volta coalition on the tower of Bulbunoso and the de Curia, this document seems a manifesto of the de Curia faction. Furthermore, on Febraury 8, 1197, after the period considered, Guglielmo Pevere declares that he owes 233 lire to the San Siro monastery. In this case a witness was Giacomo de Turca whose connections with the de Curia have been shown too.[104]

The first action of the previously mentioned Manegoldo was to destroy the 'precious palace' that Folco de Castello had in Genoa. The people involved left the city. The events are also described in one of the most impressive miniatures contained in the *Annales*, depicting Manegoldo leading the troops of the commune and directing the demolition of the de Castello house.[105] The *podestà* is the only figure riding a horse making 'visible and palpable the metaphor of ruling and riding'.[106] The picture stresses further that Ottobono saw favourably this institutional shift.

The violent reaction to the election of Manegoldo explains why Ottobono did not mention the heroic defence of Acre conducted by Folco di Castello and Guido Spinola. This aspect

---

[103] *Cassinese*, doc. 1784.

[104] *Cassinese*, doc. 211; *Le Carte*, doc. 150.

[105] *Annales*, Tav. IV, fig. 25 (reproduced below, p. 84).

[106] For the characteristics of leaders' representation see Burke, *Eyewitnessing*, pp. 59-80.

of Ottobono's narration contrasts with the *Codice Diplomatico*. In fact in every document relative to the events in the East, the names of these two individuals and the narration of their memorable actions are mentioned.[107] Most Italian cities in the same period utilised a *podestà* as a means to reach an agreement between the fighting factions. However, the transition as it occurred in Genoa was extremely different. The *podestà* was an imposition of the de Curia faction; momentarily the strongest because of the distance of its adversaries.

The reaction to the institutional reform was suffocated, and in 1191 Genoa was governed by Manegoldo.[108] The dramatic escalation of the internal tensions continued, and can be observed in the style of the author. In 1192 Ottobono again reports 'many wars ... and assaults'.[109] For 1193 the author described the violence in the city as 'a huge fire spreading in a forest ... fuelled by Satan'.[110] Ingone de Frexia was killed that year. He was consul in 1177, 1182 and 1188. Most importantly he was the son of Ingone de Volta and the father in law of Fulcone de Castello, and one of the most eminent members of the community and the leader of the de Volta coalition.[111]

The response this time was not left to isolated actions. Now the conflict rushed to its climax. The de Volta attacked during the night and conquered the new tower of the Bulbunoso family. Later, the de Curia re-conquered it.[112] The reference to this nocturnal aggression by the de Volta faction represents the last moment of the *Annales* that is characterized by a strong moral condemnation by the author. It is probable that he

---

[107] *Codice Diplomatico*, vol. II, docs. 194, 195, 196; *Codice Diplomatico*, vol. III, docs. 7, 8, 19, 20.

[108] *Annales*, p. 38.

[109] *Annales*, p. 42.

[110] *Annales*, p. 43.

[111] Olivieri, 'Cronologia', pp.199, 209, 213, states that Ingo de Frexia was the son of Ingone de Volta.

[112] *Annales*, p. 44.

Escalating Civil Conflicts

wanted to underline the fact that the de Volta attacked during the night as a cowardly action.

For 1194 his narration became almost technical; he seemed to enjoy the descriptions of the military capabilities of his citizens. A picture illustrates the battle scenes. The de Volta faction again counterattacked, their aim still being the conquest of the new tower of the Bulbunoso. To attack it, they built onto the tower of Oberto di Grimaldo and the new tower of Oberto Spinola a 'bulzone' – a flying bridge – to allow them to invade the top of the Bulbunoso's tower, which was severely damaged. However the de Curia faction responded with the construction of several war machines with which they cast stones against the Grimaldo and Spinola fortifications. The de Volta reacted in the same way, deploying war machines and hurling stones at all the proprieties of the de Curia.[113] The interpretation of this crucial passage has been thwarted by a mistaken translation that had located the de Volta on one side and the de Curia, Bulbunoso, Grimaldo and Spinola on the opposite.[114] Instead those two families were allies of the de Volta and launched the attack to the de Curia from their towers.

A translation that correctly locates the de Grimaldo and the de Spinola on the de Volta side is supported by the commercial documents and makes it possible to reinterpret these crucial events. In 1190 Oberto da Mercato mentions Oberto Spinola four times. All the documents were registered in the house of Bonifacio de Volta; in all these contracts de Volta and de Castello members appear as witnesses along with those of Spinola. The documents were all registered at the beginning of the summer 1190 and they all refer to overseas commerce financing.[115] The fact that Spinola and Grimaldo were closely

---

[113] *Annales*, p. 45.

[114] 'In 1194 ... the della Volta ... tried to demolish the tower of Bulbonoso and the towers of Spinola and Grimaldo', Moresco, 'Note' p. 223; 'The de Volta fought a proper war against the Spinola and Grimaldo', Vitale, *Il Comune*, p. 6.

[115] *Oberto 1190*, docs. 528, 642, 647, 655.

connected is demonstrated in documents dating from 1188: the two men jointly donated a church to the archbishop of Genoa.[116]

This was the most intense moment of the confrontation, and the very existence of Genoa was at risk. Ottobono wrote that the whole city did not obey the regularly elected consuls any more, and because of this the de Curia decided to nominate their own consuls: Giovanni Avvocato, Rubaldo de Curia and Enrico son of Embrione. It is interesting to notice that no condemnation is pronounced towards this action that so clearly compromised the real existence of the city.

The affiliation of the Bulbunoso family to the de Curia faction has already been demonstrated. The central role of Giovanni Avvocato inside the de Curia has been described earlier as well. Given the absence of a family name, it has not been possible to track the role of Enrico, the last man named, during the years of conflict.

At this point, the author referred to how the situation was resolved by the arrival of Markward of Anweiler in Genoa. The officer of the Emperor stated the promises of the Emperor to Genoa for its help in the conquest of Sicily. At this point, all consuls renounced their position, met for a public peace discussion and agreed to elect a *podestà*: Oberto de Olevano, from Pavia.[117] The de Volta and the de Curia gave him the 'towers of discord' in what resembles a testimony of commitment to the new peace. The newly pacified Genoa hosted the Emperor Henry VI later that year on his way to Sicily, an expedition deeply dependent on the support of Genoa's navy.

From the words of Ottobono it seemed that Markward succeeded in reaching a peace between the factions, by suggesting the very favourable concessions that the city would get if it decisively helped the Emperor in Sicily.[118] The Emperor promised to the notables of Genoa that 'the submitted Sicilian

---

[116] *Cassinese*, doc. 1492; Le Carte, docs.

[117] Represented in *Annales*, Tav. VI, fig. 34 (reproduced below, p. 86).

[118] Epstein, *Genoa*, p. 88.

kingdom was going to be not his, but of Genoa ... and not only to them but to every private citizen he gave concessions and made promises'. Indeed all these promises were already being made in 1191 as confirmed by an official document.[119]

The rest of the *Annales*, and probably its most careful part, report all the events of the easy conquest of the island. The internal events of the city had lost their central place on stage but for the last two years of the *Annales* Ottobono describes how internal peace was restored by the *podestà*.[120]

The author returned here to an unemotional style that did not identify any reason behind the conflicts that almost destroyed the city. The 'madness' that guided his citizens passed, and under the rule of the *podestà* Giacomo Manerio, in 1195, and Drudo Marcellino, in 1196, the main aim was to destroy or shorten illegal towers, that is, those which exceeded the norm of eighty feet. Drudo is described by Ottobono as 'the medicine that cured the ills of the city'. Giacomo and Drudo are also represented in two illustrations with all the formal characteristics of kings.[121] These rhetorical expressions and representations lead us to believe that it was precisely one of these *podestà* that gave the task of writing the *Annales* to Ottobono.[122]

I believe that the dramatic *crescendo* of Ottobono's description of the civil conflicts represented both the enhancement of their destructivity but also, the necessity to fully justify the role of the *podestà* and to portray them as the saviours of the commune. In fact, nothing assures the historian that Ottobono stopped to mention any conflicts in the city for the same reason.

---

[119] *Codice Diplomatico*, vol.III, doc. 2.

[120] *Annales*, p. 50.

[121] Giacomo is represented in *Annales*, Tav. VI, fig. 35; and Drudo in *Annales*, VI, fig. 37. (See below, pp. 87-88.)

[122] For the characteristics of images of rulers see Burke, *Eyewitnessing*, p. 67.

The whole documentary pool confirms the interpretation that the election of the *podestà* Manegoldo in 1190 was a move of the de Curia faction to exclude the de Volta from power. This had been possible because of the momentary weakness of the latter, as the majority of important members were fighting in the East. The reaction to this came in two acts, the first was impulsive, with the killing of Pevere in the council room, and the second carefully planned, also as a reaction to the killing of Ingone de Frexia. On this occasion the leaders of the de Volta opted for a grand-scale attack on the towers of their adversaries. They did so with a siege operation, building machines and seriously damaging their adversary's fortifications. This dramatic escalation – from battles outside the city or skirmishes on the city streets to full scale warfare inside the city walls – further confirms the interpretation that this move was very much the decision of the de Volta coalition returning to Genoa after the conclusion of the Crusade in July 1191.[123] An essential assumption of strategic culture states that an actor tends to fight a war not only in the way the external components suggest it to be fought, but also in the way the actor is best prepared to fight.[124] 'Strategies of action ... depend on habits, moods, sensibilities, and views of the world'.[125] These were all likely to had been changed by the learning experience of the Crusade.[126] Considering this, the sudden escalation in violence in 1193 is less surprising. The de Volta faction, which in this crucial moment concentrated its strength on the towers of the Spinola and Grimaldo families, fought in an organised way because they

---

[123] Vitale, *Breviario*, p. 45.

[124] For a guide to the concept of strategic culture see the 'Johnston – Gray debate': Johnston, 'Thinking about Strategic Xulture'; Gray, 'Strategic Culture as Context'; and Johnston, 'Strategic Cultures Revisited'.

[125] Swidler, 'Culture in Action', p. 277.

[126] Vitale states that the Genoese expedition astonished friends and enemies with the use of formidable siege machines. Vitale, *Breviario*, pp. 44-49.

Escalating Civil Conflicts

simply invested the knowhow of the sort of warfare that many of its members had learned defending the crusader states in the East. The experience of the Crusade relaxed the de Volta adherence to the unwritten custom that regulated the manifestations of political violence in the city.[127] The de Volta escalation paralysed the city life. This paved the way for reaching an agreement, negotiated by Markward, that lead to the election of Oberto as a new *podestà*. This time the public officer was representative of both coalitions and his election interrupted the long years of civil war. Thus the escalation realized by the de Volta coalition reached its goals. By making civil conflicts too destructive it forced a new negotiation of power in Genoa, but as we shall discuss in the next chapter it also had high costs.[128]

By now the value of the commercial contracts in defining the warring coalitions and thus in explaining the dynamics of the civil conflict is evident. With this new analysis of the sources, one which previous historians have not provided, the conflicts in Genoa do not seem to lack logic any more. The process of the struggle has emerged clearly from documents. I show in the next chapter other ways in which these commercial agreements are valuable for understanding the dynamics of the conflicts.

---

[127] Gluckman, 'The Peace', p. 1.

[128] See p. 54.

4

A CRITIQUE OF THE RECENT LITERATURE AND A POSSIBLE ECONOMICS OF CONFLICT

An analysis of the phenomenon of conflict in Genoa in the late twelfth century offers the opportunity for more general considerations. To begin, this research enables us to evaluate the most recent research regarding Genoa in that period, especially with regards to the phenomenon of conflict.

Greif's recent work on Genoa follows an 'analytic narrative approach', one that 'pays close attention to stories, accounts, and context ... is analytic in that it extracts explicit and formal lines of reasoning, which facilitate both exposition and explanation.'[129] It is an approach which has attracted fierce attacks from certain critics.[130] Greif builds an explanatory model for sophisticated historical events upon the premise of rational choice, and then proceeds to test his model with empirical evidence. His purpose is to understand the means by which institutions successfully resolved the issue of civil conflict in the past and his central example is the state-building process of Genoa.[131]

The author rightly shows that, around 1096, residents of Genoa organized themselves into a commune. He states that from 1099 to 1194, this commune was ruled by consuls, who

---

[129] Bates, *Analytic Narrative*, p. 10.

[130] A good example is Elster, 'Rational Choice History'.

[131] Greif, *Institutions*, p. 15.

were representatives of the main Genoese clans. He argues that controlling the consulate enabled a clan to gain economic benefits from the city's communal wealth. Until 1154, Greif continues, the economic gains from the control of the commune were not high enough to start an inter-clan war. The clans benefited much more from cooperating in joint piracy overseas than they would from working alone.[132] But because this cooperation enhanced Genoa's wealth, it eventually became economically beneficial to take control of the city, perhaps even through a war. Although war did not immediately break out, this was only because of the external threat of the German army of Frederick I, who had succeeded to the throne in Germany and crossed the Alps to impose the control of the Empire over the northern Italian cities. This menace reduced the potential gains open to the ruling faction. Once this menace disappeared in 1164, the clans started fighting each other. Nobody was strong enough to keep control and the civil war continued on – in different phases – for thirty years. In this reconstructed scenario both clans invested heavily in military power to prevent the other from taking control. Greif's Mutual Deterrence Model implies that this military focus drew resources away from potential economic investments. Thus the economic performance of the commune was not optimal. This dramatic situation continued until the advent – in 1194 – of a new external threat, the Italian expedition of Henry VI, the son of Frederick. At that point, a new actor appeared on the Genoese stage, a *podestà*, an external administrator who created the conditions for a peaceful period characterized by outstanding economic growth known as 'the golden age of Genoa'.[133] This particular institution ruled in Genoa for some 150 years. Here I will concentrate on the shift from the consular to the *podestaria* system as described by Greif. I proceed in this way because of

---

[132] Greif, 'On the Political Foundation'.

[133] Vitale, *Il Comune*, p. 37.

the relevance of this evolution for the civil conflicts, as already mentioned.

Greif offers a summary of this crucial passage. He describes how the German emperor Henry VI crossed the Alps with the intention of conquering Sicily, asking Genoa to give naval backing. However, the clans were involved in a fierce civil war, trying to seize the control of the Commune and thus the economic revenues of its overseas acquisitions. Consequently, the city was unable to provide this support. Henry, through his seneschal, proposed that the city accept a *podestà* as a ruler, representing the imperial authority.[134] The possibility of losing the economic gains from a Sicilian conquest and the menace of the Imperial military strength altered the balance of forces that had sunk the city into three decades of civil war and pushed the warring clans toward cooperation.

Thus the proposal was accepted. Oberto de Olivano was nominated by the Emperor to rule.[135] Under his direction, Genoese factions cooperated to support the Emperor and share the prize. The primary function of the *podestà* in Genoa was to serve as a balance of power between the warring clans, Oberto thus needed to be strong enough to ensure that no clan would be powerful enough to attempt to take power on its own, but would be weak enough to prevent him seizing total power.[136] I now reflect on the means by which Greif employs historical evidence to narrate a story that supports his institutional economic model of the transition from consular to *podestaria* government?[137] I will focus here on the empirical evidence he uses to demonstrate the robustness of his *podestaria* model, that which he uses to illustrate that the institutional change occurred through an exogenous variable – the external threat –

---

[134] Greif, *Institutions*, p. 224.

[135] In reality the Emperor recognized Genoa's autonomy in 1162, see Scarsella, *Il Comune e i Consoli*, p. 129.

[136] Greif, *Institutions*, p. 237.

[137] Greif, *Institutions*, pp. 237-238.

and that the new system was maintained because it recreated the balance of power among factions, through the military force of the *podestà*.

The first significant facet of the way in which Greif utilizes historical evidence lies in his attempt to give empirical foundation to the analytic prediction that only through an external threat Genoa could have changed its system. The confirmatory evidence provided by Greif allows him to affirm that in 1194, 'when Genoa faced a severe external threat' in the person of Henry VI, Emperor of the Holy Roman Empire,[138] the consulate was abolished and the *podestaria*, an alternative political system was established.

The evidence Greif relies on is the same *Annales* of Ottobono that I have utilised. Indeed, this – placing a great deal of emphasis on the particular political situation of the city – is an appropriate source to study the path of Genoese institutions. However, as we have previously discussed, already in 1190 the consuls had already decided to elect a *podestà*.[139] However, quite surprisingly, in the year 1191 this is not taken into consideration by Greif, although in the passage mentioned the *scriba* is clear: the government of consuls stopped and the city was ruled for the first time by a *podestà*, Manegoldo. Perhaps Greif considered this particular *podestà* not relevant in the process of state building. It is true that civil war restarted three years later. But it was relevant enough for the Annalist to stress the importance of this event, by adding an iconographic testimony to it in his work.[140] Moreover, this image has another consequence, for it implies that we should carefully question Greif's ignorance of the whole event. Indeed, he uses the beautiful miniature as one of the pictures on the cover of his book.[141]

---

[138] Greif, *Institutions*, p. 240.

[139] *Annales*, p. 37.

[140] *Annales*, Tav. IV, Fig. 25 (reproduced below, p. 84).

[141] Visible at http://www.amazon.com/dp/0521671345 (last accessed 5/5/15).

Recent Literature and Economics

Thus, although in 1190-91 Genoa was not under any particular or unexpected external threat and was 'trapped in an institutional equilibrium',[142] it did change its system. Thus a model that states the impossibility of changing the political system 'without a strong external threat'[143] is not difficult to test because of scarcity of evidence; here, it can be tested and, I argue, is found faulty.

The general impression is that – once he has built his model – Greif does not try to modify it according to the evidence, but rather the contrary. Instead of reconsidering his assumption of what were and what were not pivotal external threats, he gives the Emperor's threat absolute importance, assuming that the city did not have other serious menaces because 'the war with Pisa was conducted on the sea far away from Genoa's shore'.[144] It does not seem correct to dismiss the importance of a confrontation between two major maritime powers, whose vital interests were tied to the control of the sea, on the basis that this was fought on the sea far away from the city. Certainly these affirmations are not supported by contemporary sources, which do not characterise Pisa in the same way as Greif: a 'smaller city – that – did not pose any real threat to Genoa'.[145] Due to the lack of flexibility of his model, he prefers to convince the reader by a partial use of evidence.

The second unconvincing use of evidence relates to Greif's interpretation of the *podestà* as a military commander supported by his own men, strong enough to act as a balance of power between the leading factions in Genoa. Greif's *podestà* used his military capability to act as a deterrent towards clans willing to continue on fighting each other. He did so by making clear that he would always support the attacked faction against the attacking one, which would have been consequently

---

[142] Greif, *Institutions*, p. 224.

[143] Greif, *Institutions*, p. 237.

[144] Greif, *Institutions*, p. 44.

[145] Bates, *Analytic*, p. 36.

defeated.

The first question to pose – while considering this proposition – is related to the actual strength of the *podestà*: was he strong enough to maintain the balance?[146] Greif begins his interpretation addressing the *podestà* 'theoretically'.[147] He states the three assumptions needed to make the *podestaria* model work. First, the *podestà*, must not be militarily hegemonic, otherwise he will become a dictator. Second, he must not side with a particular faction. Third, he should reinforce inter-clan cooperation by deterring each clan from attacking another.[148] Assuming these, Greif constructs his model. Nevertheless, it is not possible to find any doubts embedded in these assumptions – and about the *podestà*'s role – in the following paragraphs. The new institutional actor, in the words of Greif, suddenly appears – as a perfectly well-known historical figure. I now analyse the evidence which allows Greif to be so assertive.

Greif affirms that the *podestà* 'was supported by twenty soldiers, two judges, and servants that he brought with him'.[149] Thus 'his – of the *podestà* – military force (possibly supported by Genoese who were unaffiliated with the main clans) was neither negligible nor considerable'.[150] These passages rely on Vitale's history of the city, but Vitale says: *'venti servi, due giudici'*[151] – twenty servants, two judges – and there is no mention at all of soldiers or fighters of any sort. Moreover, Vitale's evidence is taken from a contract relating to the *podestà* of Alba, not of Genoa.[152] Without even taking into consideration

---

[146] Clark, 'A Review', p. 740.

[147] Greif, *Institutions*, p. 324.

[148] Greif, *Institutions*, pp. 265-273.

[149] Bates, *Analytic*, p. 53.

[150] Greif, *Institutions*, p. 241.

[151] Vitale, *Il Comune*, p. 27.

[152] Vitale, *Il Comune*, p. 28.

whether an army of twenty servants was able to maintain the status quo between factions powerful enough to send to war entire fleets,[153] it seems to me that Greif pushes further his attempt to sustain his model at all costs.

Unfortunately, the whole narrative part of Greif's research, used to confirm his model, is seriously flawed, specifically by the loss of clear distinction between evidence and hypothesis, and by the numerous flaws in the analysis of evidence. I have pointed out a few examples important for their theory-destructive power, but many others could have been presented. 'The marriage of model and narrative is not easy',[154] and in this particular case, I suggest, it ended up in a painful divorce.

However Greif's work points us in the right direction; it shows the necessity of interpreting the conflict phenomenon and its connections to the city's institutional evolution. My findings differ from his. As I have shown, my hypothesis is that the shift from consular to *podestaria* system did not happen as a consequence of an external threat. The city was protagonist of external war for most of the years in which civil conflicts were fought inside its walls. The shift happened through two distinguished passages. A first one in 1190 when a *podestà* was elected as a mean to exclude the de Volta faction from power; and a second in 1194 to appease the two fighting factions. The necessity of doing so depended by the dramatic change in conducting a confrontation brought in by the de Volta coalition in 1193. This brought the de Curia to decide to share their control on the city governance.

Another value of Greif's work is that he focuses also on the economic dimension of civil conflict as well. I shall now discuss the economy of the conflict as emerged in the documents analysed. I begin by analysing the negative effects of a conflict on the healthy economic life of a community. We have already shown how the economic ties between the families were

---

[153] *Annales*, p. 42.

[154] Offer, 'Review', p. 313.

patterned on the factional ties. The following social network graph clearly evidenced this characteristic.

The economy of Genoese society reflected in its social and structure. The conflicts within the city walls were a constant aspect of the city life, even when they were not fought openly on the city street, and the economy of the city reflected this. In a sense then, I would argue that the economic loss due to the disruption of exchanges was limited. Indeed, the explosion of violence could not interrupt commercial relations because none of them were established between opposing families.

From the following graph showing the commercial ties between the families, we are offered a clearer picture of how the political division, separated also the city's economy in two distinct branches. The first one connects the families which were members of the de Curia coalition, and the second one the members of the de Volta one.

Moreover, when a conflict eventually emerged between families that were indeed connected by economic ties – as was the case for the conflicts between Navarro and Mazanello or between Grillo and Vento – we have seen that the confrontation was not brought to an extreme. We can therefore stress the role of economic ties in bringing the fighting families to a quick composition.

The same separated system emerged for the foreign policy of the city. From the commercial documents studied emerged the importance of the overseas trade for Genoa. These activities relied on the semi-colonial concessions acquired by the city. The number and relevance of these concessions depended on the role of the city as an active player on the international scene. It is widely believed that the involvement of the city in the international scene depended on the internal cohesion of Genoa.[155] In this case, too, however, we find that Genoese influence overseas was usually a matter of family politics: the commitment of specific families to the Third Crusade

---

[155] Vitale, *Il Comune*, pp. 9-11.

Recent Literature and Economics

operations is evident. As for commercial activities, then, the acquisitions of benefits overseas did not depend linearly on the level of internal peace. Indeed, Genoese individuals negotiated profitable agreements with foreign rulers utilising a consular authority which they did not have in reality, and during the period in which they were implicated in the city violence.[156] One can certainly argue that this division of foreign commitments was not the most profitable system; and, in the long run, with the growth of foreign relations, could not be sustained; but this, in the 1180s-90s at least, again reflected the conflict characteristics of the Genoese society.[157] After the election of the *podestà* Oberto in 1194, this particularity of the foreign policy started changing. At least in the words of Ottobono, the Sicilian operations involved almost the whole Genoese notables. This is one of the most evident effects of the agreement of the parties in electing a *podestà* and ending the conflicts, or at least of author's desire to leave this impression.

The separation of the factions into two independent economic systems was also maintained in the rare event of a shifting in alliances. This happened only once in the period considered and I will show how the connections between families were quickly readjusted to reflect the new situation.

The Vento family in 1183 fought alongside the de Castello family against the de Curia coalition. The social network of the Vento family in 1186 reveals a major level of trust between

---

[156] *Codice Diplomatico*, vol. II, docs. 194, 195, 196; *Codice Diplomatico*, vol. III, docs. 7, 8, 19, 20.

[157] A wonderful example of this is in Cardini, 'Profilo di un crociato'.

THE TWO FACTIONS AS EMERGED FROM THE COMMERCIAL DOCUMENTS[158]

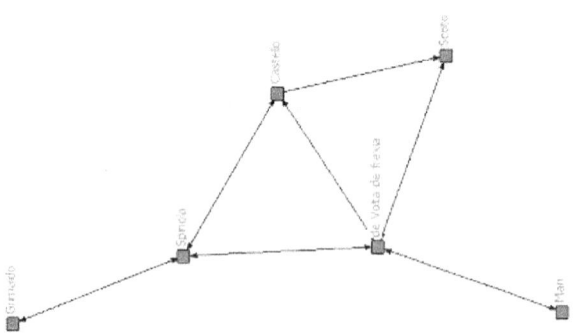

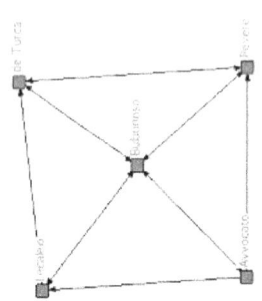

---

[158] Borgatti, *Ucinet 6*. Data from *Oberto 1186*, *Oberto 1190*, *Cassinese*, *Le Carte* and *Codice*.

Recent Literature and Economics

Vento members and de Volta members.[159] By trust, I refer to the confidence demonstrated by Vento members in spending time in de Volta buildings. Indeed almost all the documents registered by Vento's members were registered in the house of de Volta. However the only economic interest that Vento members had in common with members of the de Volta coalition were with the de Castello family. This common economic interest was also underlined by the decision of a Vento to marry a de Castello. However in 1189 these trust ties did not succeed in containing the attack of the Vento against the de Volta. The fact that this conflict was on a different level compared to the one that saw opposing each other the Grillo and the Vento in 1179, is extremely well documented by the effects that it had on the Vento–de Volta connections. The social network graph, representing the Vento network between 1190 and 1192 shows how basically all the connections between the family and the coalition stopped. This was possible because the ties depicted in the first network were not dependent on economic interest but on trust due to the family connection between Vento and de Castello. Granvotter built an analysis of networks that showed how 'small scale interaction becomes translated into large-scale patterns, and that these, feed back into small groups'.[160] Genoese family interactions seemed to be perfectly aligned to his model. Indeed 'weak' economic ties had a stronger relevance on the composition and evolution of political alliances than 'strong' family and trust ties.

VENTO SOCIAL NETWORK 1186[161] (diagram on next page)
VENTO SOCIAL NETWORK 1190-1192[162] (on page following)

---

[159] Granovetter, 'The Strength of Weak Ties', p. 1361.

[160] Granovetter, 'The Strength of Weak Ties', p. 1360.

[161] Borgatti, *Ucinet 6*. Data from *Oberto 1186* and *Le Carte*.

[162] Borgatti, *Ucinet 6*. Data from *Oberto 1190, Cassinese* and *Le Carte*.

REINTERPRETING GENOESE CIVIL CONFLICTS

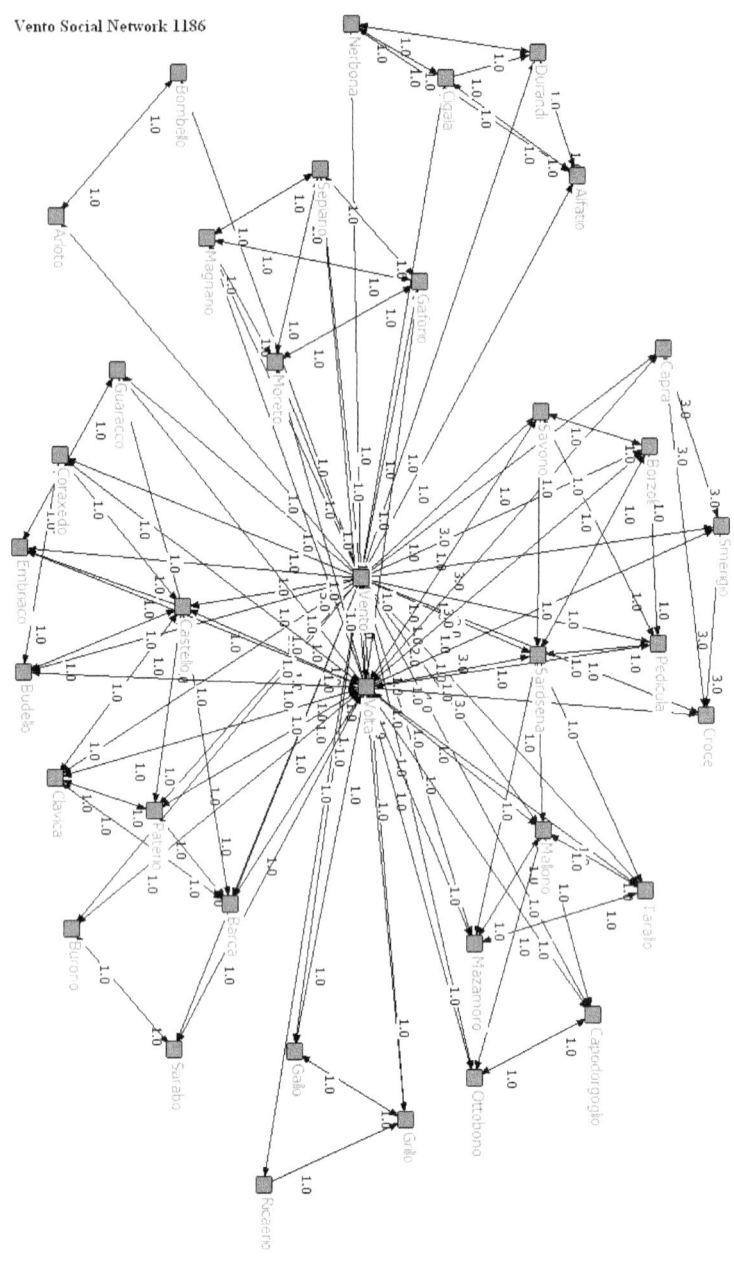

Recent Literature and Economics

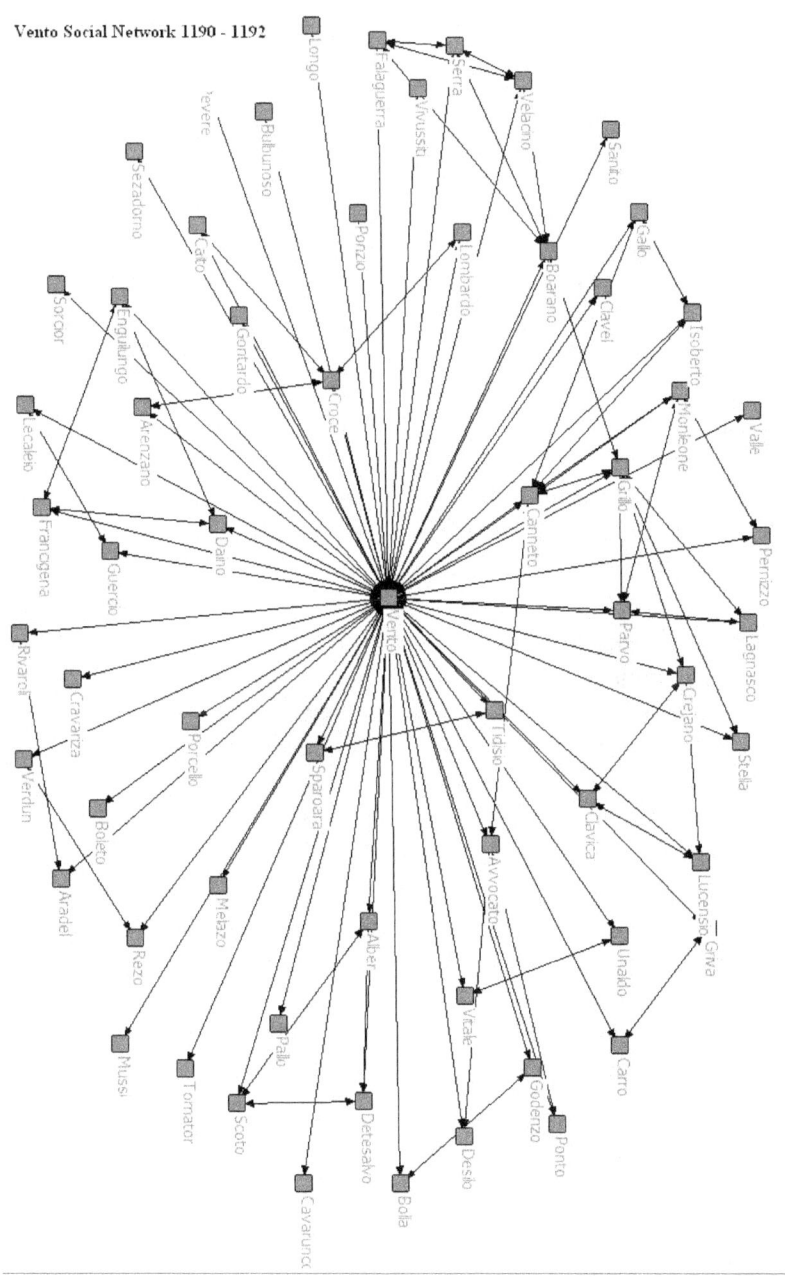

The network analysis of Granvotter is a perfect introduction to the other aspects of the economy of conflict that I am going to consider in this chapter. An aspect of the economy of conflict is certainly what Greif called the 'investment in military strength'.[163] It was certainly true that the Genoese families invested part of their wealth to ensure their security. I have shown that with the real estate transactions involving family properties. Financial capital however is not the only one invested in war. Indeed we have also noticed at the end of chapter 3, describing the implementation of the particular de Volta know how in siege warfare, that human capital was invested heavily too.[164]

However, it emerged from this research that none of the confrontations described in the *Annales* ended up with the clear victory of one of the parties. No matter how much financial capital and human capital, the factions invested in a confrontation. In other words 'the total annihilation of the enemy' was not the dominant principle of the civil conflicts under consideration.[165] The Genoese were well aware of this, and of the fact that after a fight they all had to share the same space. Emerging victorious from a confrontation did not ensure, alone, a prominent position in city politics. We have discussed in the chapters 2 and 3 that a city conflict did not receive a firm condemnation until it remained within certain boundaries and did not compromised the very integrity of the city. However we also observed that the 1193 aggression of the de Volta faction against the de Curia did not respect these unwritten rules.[166] Thus it had massive legitimacy cost on top of its physical risks. This consideration leads us to analyse another important capital that is consumed in war: social capital.[167] Particularly in this

---

[163] Greif, *Institutions*, p. 123.

[164] See p. 38.

[165] Clausewitz, *On War*, p. 228.

[166] See pp. 34-39.

[167] The literature regarding the concept of social capital is extremely vast;

Recent Literature and Economics

case the social capital lost was the one defined by Coleman, in his book *Foundation of Social Theory*, as 'the norms and the effective sanctions', accumulated by respecting the unwritten rules of a society.[168]

Legitimacy had to be rebuilt for a faction to maintain its political influence. I will now show how this was achieved by the protagonists of the 1193 escalation analysing a series of documents. In the third chapter I mentioned that in 1192 the Spinola and Grimaldo families donated a church to the archbishop of Genoa. The documents relative to the archive of the monastery of San Siro reveal the important preparatory work and the major economic investment behind this operation. Thus I assert that the operation had a political relevance, consisting in an acquisition of legitimacy by two families member of the de Volta coalition. I argue that this was an operation of 'credit slip' as described by Coleman.[169] The two families considered their operation as a kind of 'assurance'. They organised the donation of the church to the community in order to have a return in a moment of need. The operation I am going to describe was essentially conducted to build a sufficient 'credit' to be cashed in on their return.

A document of 1188 informs us that the Pope Clement III gave authorization to the archbishop of Genoa to allow the Spinola and Grimaldo families to build a chapel in the land of the San Siro monastery.[170] The negotiation then started in the year of the death of the archbishop Ugo de Volta. This is significant because the operation then was not internal to the de Volta coalition's families; the new archbishop was not a de Volta. Further, it is probable that the death of Ugo undermined the coalition's strength and legitimacy enhancing the will to act,

---

one example particularly important for the historian exploring communal Italy is Putnam, *Making Democracy Work*.

[168] Coleman, *Foundations*, p. 307.

[169] Coleman, *Foundations*, p. 317.

[170] *Le Carte*, doc. 139.

in this regard, of its members.[171] Moreover the intervention of the Pope, which was possible because of the strong political ties built by the Spinola and Grimaldo with their involvement in the Third Crusade preparations, demonstrates to the new archbishop and to the city both the power of the families and their determination. The latter is confirmed by further four documents describing the opposition that they have to face and the amount of capital invested in the operation. In fact in 1189 Clement stated that nobody was allowed to build new churches in the territory of San Siro without the permission of the abbey and monks.[172] In the same year Bonifacio, the archbishop of Genoa, conceded permission to the families to build only after they accepted to pay 12 denari annually to the Curia of the Archbishop and 20 soldi to the San Siro Monastery.[173] Finally on January 15, 1192 Oberto Spinola and Oberto Grimaldo offered the church to Archbishop Bonifacio,[174] and two weeks later Clement confirmed to Bonifacio the agreement between Oberto Spinola and the San Siro monastery for the foundation of the church.[175]

All these negotiations took place in a period of dramatic civil unrest, as we have seen, but just before the 1193 dramatic escalation. The clear political importance of this transaction is further evidenced from the *Annales*: Ottobono did not mention the foundation of this church, just as he did not mention the glorious actions of the same families in the East, probably for the same reason mentioned before. Moreover the fact that the pope Celestine only in July 1197 gave mandate to Bonifacio to dissolve the two families from the obligation of paying 20 soldi every year to the monastery of San Siro, stresses further the economic burden of this operation for families that in the very

---

[171] On the concept of legitimacy see Schiera, 'Legitimacy'.

[172] *Le Carte*, doc. 138.

[173] Olivieri, 'Serie dei Consoli', p. 386.

[174] *Cassinese*, doc. 1492.

[175] *Le Carte*, doc. 193.

same years were involved in a dramatic confrontation.[176] Such an investment had surely a political meaning that could not have been separated by the events happening in the city at the same moment.

The declared aim of this operation was religious. Clement III conceded the building of the church 'for the soul' of Oberto Spinola. We have already seen in the *Annales* how the vocabulary of religion infused the political dimension of conflict in Genoa. The reference to the political climate of the city is far clearer in other passages of this operation. One document states the impossibility for the families Spinola and Grimaldo to go safely to the mass in San Siro. This is declared as one of the reason for the foundation of the new church. Moreover it is stated that even their family burials needed a safer place. All of these were clear political messages to claim the victim status of these families, just before of their ultimate attack.[177]

---

[176] *Le Carte*, doc. 152.

[177] *Le Carte*, doc. 139.

Conclusion

I wanted to use this research to outline the need of a new analysis of the phenomenon of civil conflicts in communal Italy. I have taken in consideration the civil conflicts in Genoa described in the *Annales* of Ottobono between 1174 and 1196.

At the outset, the study was premised on refusing to believe that civil conflicts in the twelfth century are impossible to be interpreted rationally and that it is illusory to divide the fighting families into well defined factions for the period. Thus I have conducted a careful analysis of the *Annales* in the light of the valuable commercial records of the city. This operation showed the deep political and economic characteristics of civil conflicts as theorized by Zorzi and Greif. The works of Zorzi argue for the political relevance of civil conflicts in the cities of communal Italy, and the works of Greif show that the economic aspects of civil conflicts could not have been ignored further. Violence emerged as one of the most important characteristics of the city life. When it was utilised within established limits it was a legitimate mean of political confrontation and it shaped the economic structure of the city.

Genoa appeared to be divided between two main factions that used violence as one of the bargaining elements of political discourse. Utilising extensive commercial records it has been possible to locate successfully the families involved in the civil conflicts inside the two opposing coalitions: de Volta and de Curia. In fact what emerged from the sources is an economic system split into two branches, reflecting the political factions. Thus it is possible to outline how the society of Genoa was clearly shaped by civil conflicts even during the years in which they did not happen.

This study provided me with the necessary tools to understand what lead to the final escalation of the conflict in 1190-94, when violence reached such an unprecedented level.

Moreover, the works of Greif remind us of the necessity of linking any interpretation of historical events firmly to the evidence available. I think that this has been showed clearly in this paper. It corrected some mistakes that had been committed by valid historians while venturing in a territory that of Genoese civil conflicts which is difficult given the complexity of the sources available to explore it.

I believe that the importance of the economic components of civil conflicts and, with careful use of the explanatory value of the sources I built what can be regarded as an economy of conflict. I dealt with the ways in which economic actors prtected their affairs from the conflicts, and I have shown how families allocated various types of capitals in the machine of civil conflicts.

Analysing the civil conflicts that afflicted Genoa in the two decades considered, under the light of different evidence, they appeared to be an essential feature of Genoese society both from the political and economic perspectives.

AFTERWORD

This book explored in detail the chronicle of *Ottobonus scriba* to examine the phenomenon of civil violence in Genoa in the late twelfth century. In focusing on one Genoese chronicle it contributed to the broader developments of economic and political history.

As we have seen in the introduction, the historiographical fate of the Genoese civil conflicts of the period is a fascinating one. While their importance for the survival of the communal institutions has been frequently underlined, they have often been ignored in the historiography.

This absence emerges in reading the existing global histories of Genoa – aiming to offer as complete a picture as possible of the political, social and economic development of the city.

The last work of the eminent Genoese historian Vito Vitale, the 1955 *Breviario della storia di Genova*, the 1968 *Storia di Genova* of Teofilo Ossian de Negri, and the 1996 *Genoa and the Genoese*, by Steven Epstein,[178] all refer to the civil conflicts that

---

[178] Paola Guglielmotti refers to the work of Epstein as the '1996 contribution of an American author ... who nonetheless remains decisively faithful to the interpretative lines traced before him and that proceeds by anchoring his work to the sequence of events', Guglielmotti, 'La storia medievale. Parte II (1960-2007)', in Puncuh, D. (ed.), *La Società Ligure di Storia Patria nella Storiografia Italiana, 1857-2007* (Genova, 2010), p. 157. Guglielmotti also published a review of Epstein's work in *Studi medievali*. However, it must also be acknowledged, to use the words of David Abulafia on the back cover of the book, that '[t]his book fills a gaping hole in the literature ... at long last giving its due to a city-state that played a central role in the political and economic history of the Mediterranean'. The importance of the works of Vitale and De Negri as a

raged in the city, respectively as a 'chaos of clashes', 'facts that repeat themselves in never ending and ever changing patterns', and 'bouts of self destruction'.[179] Vitale justifies his brevity by stressing that '[e]very attempt of giving order to the chaos of clashes ... appears as a desperate endeavour'.[180] Vitale's decision to essentially leave out of his study an analysis of twelfth century conflict gravely undermines his own work because stating that 'the *podestarial* government, almost unconsciously, had risen to put an end to those *risse nobiliari* – aristocratic brawls', he seems to admit that these brawls are deserving of further attention.[181] De Negri, following in Vitale's footsteps, warns that 'an attempt to uncover the origins and reconstruct the events of these contrasts would be a vain effort, mostly because of the scarcity of the sources. [People] [w]ho attempted to shed more light on these events ... eventually renounced the endeavor...'.[182] Epstein largely overlooks this phenomenon on the basis that '[p]erhaps all sorts of people were knifing each other on the streets; the chronicle records assaults on and by important people because of the stir such events caused, not because they reflected deep political disputes among the elite'. However, he concedes that 'the increasing role of factionalism in Genoese politics is uncontestable' and reflects on the fact

---

starting point is recognized by Puncuh in his preface to Puncuh, D. (ed.), *La Società Ligure*. Paola Guglielmotti, speaking of the lack of recent attempts to write a much needed renewed comprehensive history of the city refers to 'a carefulness to formulate comprehensive visions on behalf of the Genoese academic community', 'La storia medievale. Parte II (1960-2007)', p. 157, in Puncuh (ed.), *La Società Ligure*.

[179] Vitale, *Breviario*, p. 29; De Negri, *Storia di Genova* (Firenze, 2003), p. 304; Epstein, S., *Genoa and the Genoese, 958–1528*, p. 80.

[180] Vitale, *Breviario.*, p. 29.

[181] Vitale, *Il comune del Podestà a Genova* (Milano, 1951), pp. 9-10.

[182] De Negri, *Storia di Genova*, p. 304. The aim of the work of De Negri is 'to fill the lacuna left by Vitale', Puncuh, *Storia di Genova: Mediterraneo, Europa, Atlantico* (Genova, 2003), p. 6.

Afterword

that the 'faction-plagued elite [was] discredited by its pointless violence', clearly acknowledging, in contrast to Vitale or de Negri, that the disputes did have deep political and social consequences and were therefore deserving of more attention.[183]

The first contribution of this book therefore is to start changing this image of an unfathomable phenomenon. Internal violence emerges in this text as an historical phenomenon that can be studied in its development, if the sources are fully explored.

Partly as a consequence of this gap in the historiography, recent attempts to uncover the dominant motives behind Genoese civil conflicts in the twelfth and early thirteenth centuries are plagued by a misrepresentation of the often-conflictual relations between the families forming the city's elite. I am referring here to the works of Gerald Day and Avner Greif, which had to rely on the traditional reconstruction of the twelfth century consular elite in Genoa. In this view, the violent episodes in Genoa were originated by a contraposition between two well-defined clans opposing one another. These clans developed, it is believed, from the division of the family of the viscounts that ruled over Genoa in the Carolingian period. In the words of Steven Epstein: 'The family of the viscounts of Genoa had split into three main branches: the *de Caramandino*, *de Insulis* (delle Isole), and *Manesseno* lines'.[184] Accepting this

---

[183] Epstein, *Genoa and the Genoese*, pp. 108, 75 and 138.

[184] Epstein, *Genoa and the Genoese*, p. 75. The genealogical reconstructions at the base of this interpretation were proposed for the first time in Tommaso Belgrano, 'Tavole genealogiche a corredo della illustrazione del registro arcivescovile', tables (hereinafter, tav.) 19-38. I quote from Epstein because I want to stress the fact that these nineteenth century reconstructions are still widely believed, or at least used. In chapter three I consider the validity of such reconstructions more carefully. Here I would like to stress that building on the doubts formulated by Giovanna Petti Balbi (see I *Visconti*), Luca Filangieri in his dissertation has most recently attempted to evaluate critically the genealogical reconstructions of Belgrano at the basis of this supposed division of the city in two well defined factions, 'Famiglie e gruppi dirigenti a Genova',

assumption, Day and Greif focused on the potential motives that animated this contraposition.[185]

Gerald Day, in his *Genoa's Response to Byzantium*, hypothesizes that the families of the *de Manesseno* branch were expansionist in policy, and were opposed by the families of the *de Carmadino* branch who were in contrast conservative.[186] Epstein concedes that the hypothesis of Day 'makes sense', and underlines that Day's 'complicated argument sometimes depends on tenuous evidence ... [b]ut it is the best explanation for factions in Genoa'. On the other hand, Epstein stresses that '[p]ersonal and familial rivalries, based on envy rather than policy differences, cannot be excluded as an impetus to factionalism; nor can a crass desire for power'.[187] Avner Greif's work is much more ambitious in scope, however, precisely the latter motivation, 'a crass desire for power', can be essentially considered as the basis of Avner Greif's interpretation of civil conflict in Genoa in the twelfth and thirteenth century. The scholar – again relying on preexisting interpretations – argues that 'there are two clans – in Genoa – with infinite life-spans'. Each one of them can decide 'whether to attack the other' in order to become 'a "controlling clan", which receives all future income...' or to cooperate in the joint administration of the

---

pp. 8-37. Filangieri's brilliant contribution – in my opinion – must radically change the use that has been made of the works of Belgrano, which appear seriously undermined by their reliance on very little historical evidence.

[185] Between *de Carmadino* and *de Manesseno*, for in this interpretation the 'clan d'Isola was not politically active'; see e.g. Greif, *Institutions*, p. 224.

[186] Day, G. W., *Genoa's Response to Byzantium, 1155-1204: Commercial Expansion and Factionalism in a Medieval City* (Urbana, 1988), p. 10. Day investigates Genoese conflicts by focusing on how Genoa's relations with Byzantium played a role in the emergence of factionalism in Genoa; and, vice-versa, how internal politics in Genoa would sometimes profoundly affect the diplomatic situation, *ibid.*, pp. 70-107.

[187] Epstein, *Genoa and the Genoese*, pp. 75 and 76 and p. 336, note 61.

Afterword

city.[188] According to the author, internal peace would be maintained as long as the gains received from becoming a controlling clan remained sufficiently low; and in turn those were to remain low as long as the threat of internal war was consistent. Therefore, Greif believes, 'under a mutual-deterrence equilibrium, peace comes at the price of economic prosperity'.[189] Although trapped in this equilibrium, the clans eventually started to cooperate because of 'an unexpected parametric change' which appeared in the figure of the external threat from the German emperor Frederick I Barbarossa.[190] Thanks to this external threat, the Genoese cooperated and the city grew richer; as a consequence 'controlling the consulate was more profitable' and 'theory predicts that Genoa's clans were more likely to challenge each other militarily'. A civil war ensued and it was stopped only by an institutional development that 'enabled the Genoese to end the civil war, further mobilize their resources, and attain a new level of economic prosperity'. Greif identifies this development in the transition from the consular commune to the *podestarial* one.[191] In order to do so Greif theorizes that the *podestà* in Genoa fostered inter-clan cooperation by creating a balance of power. Avner Offer, commenting on Greif's work, warns us that 'the marriage of model and narrative is not easy'.[192] In a sense Avner Greif's work demonstrates the pressing necessity for an interpretation of Genoese civil conflicts solidly grounded in the vast evidence available.

---

[188] Greif, *Institutions*, pp. 224-225.

[189] Greif, *Institutions*, p. 225.

[190] Greif, *Institutions*, p. 233.

[191] Greif, *Institutions*, pp. 234-236.

[192] Offer, 'Review' in *The Journal of Economic History*, 60:1 (2000), p. 313.

In filling this gap in the historiography, therefore, this book shows the possibilities of an interpretation of Genoese civil conflicts much more grounded in the historical evidence.

Furthermore, this book contributes to the much wider debate on the role played by civil conflicts in the development of medieval societies and institutions – well beyond the walls of medieval Genoa.

Indeed this phenomenon should be considered a crucial one, both on its own, and for its implications for the development of the economic and political trajectories of the northern Italian communes.[193]

The theme of conflict in urban societies in the Middle Ages and Early Modern Period is at the same time one that is currently at the center of debate internationally, but one that has been applied only with difficulty to the political experience of the communes in northern and central Italy.[194]

The interests of medievalists that specialize on this time period have mostly focused on the origins and social profiles of the elites of the communes, on the production and creation of documents and archives by these societies, and finally on the communes as theatres of development of a political culture which had varied influences. Crucially, then, the prevailing interpretation of the communal experience has been a public

---

[193] Zorzi, A., 'I conflitti nell'Italia comunale: Riflessioni sullo stato degli studi e sulle prospettive della ricerca', in *Conflitti: Pace e Vendetta Nell'Italia Comunale*, ed. A. Zorzi (Firenze, 2009).

[194] From the very rich bibliography accumulated in recent years we should remember the collective efforts: *Disputes and Settlements: Law and Human Relations in the West*, ed. J. Bossy (Cambridge, 1983); *The Peace of God: Social Violence and Religious Response in France Around the Year 1000*, eds. T. F. Head and R. Landes (Ithaca, 1992); *La Giustizia Nell'Alto Medioevo, Secoli IX-XI* , ed. Centro Italiano di studi sull'alto Medioevo (Spoleto, 1997); *The Conflict in Medieval Europe: Changing Perspectives on Society and Culture*, eds. W. C. Brown and P. Górecki (Aldershot, 2003); *Conflitti: Pace e Vendetta Nell'Italia Comunale*, ed. A. Zorzi (Firenze, 2009).

Afterword

one. Recently the focus of the analysis has been on the modes of political participation, the exclusion from political participation, and the development of various types of councils, the application of new charters, the progressive growth of the public functions in judicial and fiscal matters and so forth.

The particular direction in the tendencies of the current research focuses essentially on themes that appear to be directed against the more recent focus of political history. The latter demonstrated a strong focus on renewing objects of analysis and perspectives, essentially away from diplomatic history and official political history, to analyse political and social developments in their complex and informal dimensions.

This book, using the private commercial agreements of the Genoese citizens, has indicated a direction to change this picture, by focusing on the economic aspects of civil conflict.

The Italian communes, instead, have been prevalently seen as political incubators for the structures of the future states. The profile of the commune as the prototypical "city-state" is well rooted in the recent analysis, especially the ones from Italian scholars. In the words of Andrea Zorzi, the Italian communes seem to be "public islands" in an international historiographical debate that underlines the complexities and the varieties of these political and social experiences.

What can explain the delay of the development of an innovative approach to the study of conflicts in the Italian communes? It is noteworthy that in his collection of essays on the issue of violence in late Medieval Italian cities, Lauro Martines complains that 'the absence of a paper on Genoa ... the collection's major lacuna' is due to the impossibility of 'find[ing] an expert prepared to write an essay on the subject'.[195]

---

[195] Martines, L. (ed.), *Violence and Civil Disorder in Italian Cities, 1200-1500* (Berkeley and Los Angeles, 1972), p. 18.

This state of affairs has yet to change and if the whole subject of political violence is still an obscure one, then medieval Genoa is its less studied aspect. This research demonstrates that this impasse can be solved in several ways.

This book gave a brief introduction into this more holistic approach to the study of medieval conflict and, I believe, shows how a deeper interpretation of the phenomenon of conflict in medieval Genoa is possible.

Initially, it is necessary to understand how the practice of conflict left traces in a number of documentary sources. As we have seen through the book, the notary material that survived until today can be utilized to shed light on the practices of conflict and on the structures of the factions that participated.

Furthermore, through a careful reading of the chronicles clear differences emerge in both the phases and the perceptions of violence. These differences appeared essentially on two fronts. First, it is necessary to distinguish the variety and intensity of the different phases of conflict. Secondly, the size and status of the groups that participated in conflicts also contribute to our understanding of the phenomenon as one that developed in time. My current research aims to do just that, working towards the deepening of our understanding of the phenomenon of civil conflict and its consequences on the political and economic development of medieval and early modern societies.

Finally, the book contributes to the economic history discipline beyond the phenomenon of civil conflict. As has been discussed, the city of Genoa has, for a long time, captured the attention of economic historians interested in uncovering the reasons behind its economic successes. This city has been repeatedly considered the birthplace of capitalism and of finance, and one of the Italian cities that led the way for western European worldwide economic dominance, to the point that Roberto Sabatino Lopez formulated his theory

Afterword

of a late medieval commercial revolution, from his studies of Genoa.[196]

This book is a first attempt to include again in our analysis of the Genoese economy the impact of the social and political relations that were active within the city walls. In shedding light on the structures and development of the Genoese economy through an informed analysis of the notary documents, the book demonstrated that it is possible to utilize the surviving records to reconstruct the role played by economic connections in the development of the Genoese society.

---

[196] Lopez, R. S., *The Commercial Revolution of the Middle Ages, 950-1350* (Cambridge, 1976).

BIBLIOGRAPHY

Primary Sources

Annali Genovesi di Caffaro e de' suoi continuatori dal MXCIX al MCCXCIII, eds. BELGRANO, L. T. and IMPERIALE, C. (Roma, 1890-1901).

Archivio Durazzo-Giustiniani, Via Balbi 1, 16126 Genova, ed. FILANGIERI, L. (Genova, unpublished).

Archivio Segreto, in *Archivio di Stato di Genova*, Piazza S. Leonardo 3, 16128 Genova, ed. FILANGIERI, L. (Genova, unpublished).

Codice Diplomatico della Repubblica di Genova, ed. IMPERIALE, C., (Roma, 1936).

Guglielmo Cassinese 1190-1192, eds. HALL, M., HILMAR, C. and REYNOLDS, L. (Genova, 1938).

Le Carte del Monastero di San Siro di Genova dal 952 al 1224, eds. BASILI, A., and POZZA, L. (Genova, 1974).

Il Cartolare di Giovanni Scriba, eds. CHIAUDANO, M., and MORESCO, M. (Roma, 1935).

Oberto Scriba de Mercato, 1186, ed. CHIAUDANO (Genova, 1940).

Oberto Scriba de Mercato, 1190, eds. M. CHIAUDANO and R. MOROZZO della ROCCA (Torino, 1938).

Secondary Sources

ABULAFIA, D., *The Two Italies* (Cambridge, 1977).

AIRALDI, G., and KEDAR, B. (eds.), *I Comuni Italiani nel Regno Crociato di Gerusalemme* (Genova, 1986).

AIRALDI, G., *Comuni e Signorie nell'Italia Settentrionale: Il Piemonte e la Liguria*, in GALASSO, G. (ed.), *Storia d'Italia*, vol. 5, (Torino, 1987).

CIPOLLA, C. M., *Storia Economica dell'Europa pre-industriale* (Bologna, 1974).

BACH, E., *La citè de Genes au XII siècle.*

BATES, R., GREIF, A., LEVI, M., ROSENTHAL, J., and WEINGAST, B., *Analytic Narratives* (Princeton, 1998).

BATES, R., GREIF, A., and SINGH, S., 'Organising Violence', *The Journal of Conflict Resolution*, 46, 5, 2002, pp. 599-628.

BORGATTI, S. P., EVERETT, M. G., and FREEMAN, L. C., *UCINET 6 for Windows* (Harvard, 2002).

BORGATTI, S. P., EVERETT, M. G., and FREEMAN, L. C., *UCINET 6 for Windows: User's Guide* (Harvard, 2002).

BOSSY, J. (ed.), *Dispute and Settlements: Law and Human Relations in the West* (Cambridge, 1983).

BRACE, P., COHEN, Y., GRAY, V., and LOWERY, D., 'How Much Do Interest Groups Influence State Economic Growth?', *The American Political Science Review*, 83, 4, 1989, pp. 1297-1308.

BROWN, W. C., and GÓRECKI, P. (eds.), *The Conflict in Medieval Europe: Changing Perspectives on Society and Culture* (Aldershot, 2003).

BURKE, P., *Eyewitnessing: The Uses of Images as Historical Evidence* (London, 2001).

CAPOCCIA, G., and KELEMEN, R., 'The Study of Critical Junctures: Theory, Narrative and Counterfactuals in Historical Institutionalism', *World Politics*, 59, 3, 2007, pp. 341-369.

CARDINI, F., 'Profilo di un crociato: Guglielmo Embriaco', *Archivio storico italiano*, 136, 1978, pp. 405-436.

Bibliography

CASARETTO, P. F., 'La Moneta Genovese', in *Atti della Società Ligure*, Vol. 55 (Genova, 1928).

CENTRO ITALIANO di studi sull'alto Medioevo (ed.), *La Giustizia Nell'Alto Medioevo, Secoli IX-XI* (Spoleto, 1997).

CHIFFOLEAU, J., GAUVARD, C., and ZORZI, A. (eds.), *Pratiques Sociales et Politiques Judiciaires* (Roma, 2007).

CHITTOLINI, G., 'The "Private," the "Public," the State', *The Journal of Modern History*, 67, 1995, pp. 34-61.

CLARK, G. 'A Review of Avner Greif's Institutions and the Path to the Modern Economy: Lessons from Medieval Trade', *Journal of Economic Literature*, 45, 2007, pp. 727-743.

CLAUSEWITZ, C., *On War* (London, 1968).

COLEMAN, J. S., *Foundations of Social Theory* (Cambridge, 1990).

DAVID, P., 'Path Dependence – A Foundational Concept for Historical Social Science', *The Journal of Historical Economics and Econometric History*, 1, 2, 2007, pp. 1-20.

DAY, G. W., *Genoa's Response to Byzantium, 1155-1204: Commercial Expansion and Factionalism in a Medieval City* (Urbana, 1988).

DE NEGRI, T., *Storia di Genova* (Firenze, 2003).

DE ROOVER, F. E., 'The Business Records of an Early Genoese Notary, 1190-1192', *Bulletin of Business Historical Society*, 14, 3, 1940, pp. 41-46.

DEAN, T., 'Marriage and Mutilation: Vendetta in Late Medieval Italy', *Past and Present*, 157, 1, 1997, pp. 3-36.

DOUGLASS, C., and THOMAS, P., *The Rise of the Western World* (New York, 1973).

ELSTER, J., 'Rationality, Morality, and Collective Action', *Ethics*, 96, 1, 1985, pp. 136-155.

ELSTER, J., 'Social Norms and Economic Theory', *The Journal of Economic Perspectives*, 3, 4, 1989, pp. 99-117.

ELSTER, J. 'Review: Rational Choice History: A Case of Excessive Ambition', *The American Political Science Review*, 94, 3, 2000, pp. 685-695.

EPSTEIN, S., *Wills and Wealth in Medieval Genoa, 1150-1250* (Cambridge, 1984).

EPSTEIN, S., *Genoa and the Genoese, 958–1528* (Chapel Hill and London, 1996).

FACE, R., 'Secular History in XII Century Italy: Caffaro of Genoa', *Journal of Medieval History*, 6, 2, 1980, pp. 169-184.

FENOALTEA, S., 'Slavery and Supervision in Comparative Perspective: A Model', *The Journal of Economic History*, 44, 3, 1984, pp. 635-668.

FILANGIERI, L., *Famiglie e gruppi dirigenti a Genova (secoli XII-metà XIII)*, doctoral dissertation, Università degli Studi di Firenze, 2010.

FREUND, J., *The Sociology of Max Weber* (London, 1968).

GLUCKMAN, M., 'The Peace in the Feud', *Past and Present*, 8, 1955, pp. 1-14.

GOITEIN, S. D., 'Geniza Papers of a Documentary Character in the Gaster Collection of the British Museum', *The Jewish Quarterly Review*, New Ser., 51, 1, 1960, pp. 34-46.

GOITEIN, S. D., *A Mediterranean Society: Economic Foundations* (Los Angeles, 1967).

GOITEIN, S. D., *A Mediterranean Society: The Community* (Los Angeles, 1971).

GOITEIN, S. D., *Letters of Medieval Jewish Traders* (Princeton, 1973).

GRANOVETTER, M., 'The Strength of Weak Ties', *The American Journal of Sociology* 78, 6, 1973, pp. 1360-1380.

GRANOVETTER, M., 'Economic Action and Social Structure: The Problem of Embeddedness', *The American Journal of Sociology*, 91,

Bibliography

3, 1985, pp. 481-510.

GREIF, A., *Institutions and the Path to the Modern Economy: Lessons from Medieval Trade* (Cambridge, 2006).

GREIF, A., 'Reputation and coalitions in Medieval Trade: Evidence on the Maghribi Traders', *Journal of Economic History*, 49, 4, 1989, pp. 857-882.

GREIF, A., 'The Organization of Long-Distance Trade: Reputation and Coalitions in the Geniza Documents and Genoa During the XI and XII Centuries', *The Journal of Economic History*, 51, 2, 1991, pp. 459-462.

GREIF, A., 'Institution and Commitment in International Trade: Lessons from the Commercial Revolution', *American Economic Review*, 82, 2, 1992, pp. 128-133.

GREIF, A., 'Contract enforceability and Economic Institutions in Early Trade: The Maghribi Traders' Coalition', *American Economic Review*, 83, 3, 1993, pp. 525-548.

GREIF, A., 'On the Political Foundations of the Late Medieval Commercial Revolution: Genoa during the XII and XIII Centuries', *Journal of Economic History*, 54, 4, 1994, pp. 271-287.

GREIF, A., 'Political Organizations, Social Structures, and Institutional Success: Reflection from Genoa and Venice during the Commercial Revolution', *Journal of Institutional and Theoretical Economics*, 151, 4, 1995, 734-740.

GRENDI, E., *Profilo storico degli alberghi genovesi* (Roma, 1975).

GUGLIELMOTTI, P., 'La storia medievale: Parte II (1960-2007)', in PUNCUH, D. (ed.), *La Società Ligure di Storia Patria nella Storiografia Italiana, 1857-2007* (Genova, 2010), p. 157.

HEAD, T. F., and LANDES, R. (eds.), *The Peace of God: Social Violence and Religious Response in France Around the Year 1000* (Ithaca, 1992).

HEERS, J., *Le livre des comptes de Giovanni Piccamiglio home d'affaires genois* (Paris, 1961).

HEERS, J., *Le clan familial au moyen age* (Paris, 1977).

HEERS, J., *Parties and Political life in the Medieval West* (Amsterdam, New York, Oxford, 1977).

HOOVER, C. B., 'The Sea Loan in Genoa in the Twelfth Century', *The Quarterly Journal of Economics*, 40, 3, 1926, pp. 495-529.

HYDE, J., *Society and Politics in Medieval Italy* (London, 1973).

HUGHES, D. O., 'Urban Growth and Family Structure in Medieval Genoa', *Past and Present*, 66, 1, 1975, pp. 3-28.

HUGHES, D. O., 'Il matrimonio nell'Italia medievale', in DE GIORGIO, M., and KLAPISCH-ZUBER, C., *Storia del matrimonio* (Roma-Bari, 1996).

LANE, F., *Venice: A Maritime Republic* (Baltimore, 1973).

LEWIS, A., *Naval Power and Trade in the Mediterranean. A.D. 500-1100* (Princeton 1951).

LEWIS, A., and RUNYAN, T., *European Naval and Maritime History, 300-1500* (Bloomington, 1985).

LOPEZ, R. S., *Storia delle colonie genovesi nel Mediterraneo* (Bologna, 1938).

LOPEZ, R. S., 'European Merchants in the Medieval Indies', *Journal of Economic History*, 3, 1, 1993, pp. 164-188.

LOPEZ, R. S., *The Commercial Revolution of the Middle Ages, 950-1350* (Cambridge, 1976).

MAIRE VIGUEUR, J. C., *Cittadini e Cavalieri* (Firenze, 2004).

MAIRE VIGUEUR, J. C., *I Podesta` dell'Italia Comunale* (Roma, 2000).

MARTINES, L. (ed.), *Violence and Civil Disorder in Italian Cities, 1200-1500* (Berkeley and Los Angeles, 1972).

McGOVERN, J., 'The Documentary Language of Medieval Business, A.D. 1150-1250', *The Classical Journal*, 67, 3, 1972, pp. 227-239.

Bibliography

MOLHO, A., 'Review: Parties and Political Life in The Medieval West', *The American Historical Review*, 84, 1, 1979, p. 134.

MORESCO, M., and BOGNETTI, G. P., *Per l'edizione dei notai liguri del sec. XII* (Torino, 1938).

MORESCO, M., 'Note sulla fondazione della chiesa gentilizia degli Spinola nel 1188 in Genova', in *Studi di Storia e Diritto in onore di Enrico Besta per il XL anno del suo insegnamento*, vol. 4 (Milano, 1939).

OFFER, A., 'Going to War in 1914: A Matter of Honor?', *Politics & Society*, 23, 2, 1995, pp. 213-241.

OFFER, A., 'Review', *The Journal of Economic History*, 60, 1, 2000, pp. 312-314.

OLIVIERI, A., 'Cronologia dei Consoli del Comune di Genova', in *Atti della Società Ligure* (Genova, 1878), p. 213.

OLSON, M., *The Rise and Decline of Nations* (New Haven, 1982).

OTTERBEIN, K., 'Internal War: A Cross-Cultural Study', *American Anthropologist*, New Series, 70, 2, 1968, pp. 277-289.

PETTI BALBI, G., *Genova medievale vista dai contemporanei* (Genova, 1979).

PETTI BALBI G., 'Magnati e Popolani in area ligure', in *Magnati e Popolani nell'Italia comunale*, Atti del XV convegno di studi del Centro Italiano di studi di storia e d'arte (Pistoia, 1997), pp. 243-272.

PETTI BALBI, G., *Governare la citta`: pratiche sociali e linguaggi politici a Genova in eta` medievale* (Firenze, 2007).

PRYOR, J., *Geography, Technology, and War* (Cambridge, 1988).

PUNCUH, D., *Storia di Genova: Mediterraneo, Europa, Atlantico* (Genova, 2003).

PUNCUH, D. (ed.), *La Società Ligure di Storia Patria nella Storiografia Italiana, 1857-2007* (Genova, 2010).

PUTNAM, R. D., Leonardi, R., and Nanetti, R. Y., *Making Democracy Work* (Princeton, 1993).

RAGGIO, O., *Faide e Parentele* (Torino, 1990).

ROBERTS, S., *Order and Dispute: An Introduction to Legal Anthropology* (London, 1979; since reprinted, 2d ed., New Orleans, 2013).

SCARSELLA, A., *Il Comune dei Consoli*, vol.III of *Storia di Genova dalle origini al tempo nostro* (Milano, 1942).

SCHIERA, P., 'Legitimacy, Discipline, and Institutions: Three Necessary Conditions for the Birth of the Modern State', *The Journal of Modern History*, 67, 1995, pp. 511-533.

SCHWARZ, R., 'Two Sources of Medieval Business History', *The American Journal of Legal History*, 2, 3, 1958, pp. 237-255.

SWIDLER, A. 'Culture in Action: Symbols and Strategies', *American Sociological Review*, 51, 2, 1986, pp. 273-286.

TABACCO, G., *The Struggle for Power in Medieval Italy* (Cambridge, 1989).

TABACCO, G., 'Il tema della famiglia e del suo funzionamento nella società medievale', *Quaderni storici*, 11, 1976.

TVERSKY, A., and KAHNEMAN, D., 'Judgment under Uncertainty', *Science*, New Series, 185, 4157, 1974, pp. 1124-1131.

VITALE, V., *Il comune del podestà a Genova* (Milano, 1951).

VITALE, V., *Breviario della Storia di Genova* (Genova, 1955).

WHITE, S. D., *Feuding and Peace-Making in Eleventh-Century France* (London, 2005).

WICKHAM, C., 'Review: Systactic Structures: Social Theory for Historians', *Past and Present*, 132, 1991, pp. 188-203.

WICKHAM, C., *Courts and Conflict in Twelfth-century Tuscany* (Oxford, 2004).

YORAM, B., 'The F-Connection: Families, Friends, and Firms and the Organization of Exchange', *Population and Development Review*, 6, 1, 1980, pp. 1-30.

Bibliography

ZORZI, A., 'La cultura della vendetta nel conflitto politico in età comunale', in DELLE DONNE, R., and ZORZI, A. (eds.), *Le storie e la memoria* (Firenze, 2002).

ZORZI, A. (ed.), *Conflitti: Pace e Vendetta Nell'Italia Comu¬nale* (Firenze, 2009).

ZORZI, A., 'I conflitti nell'Italia comunale: Riflessioni sullo stato degli studi e sulle prospettive della ricerca', in ZORZI, A. (ed.), *Conflitti: Pace e Vendetta Nell'Italia Comunale* (Firenze, 2009).

APPENDIX

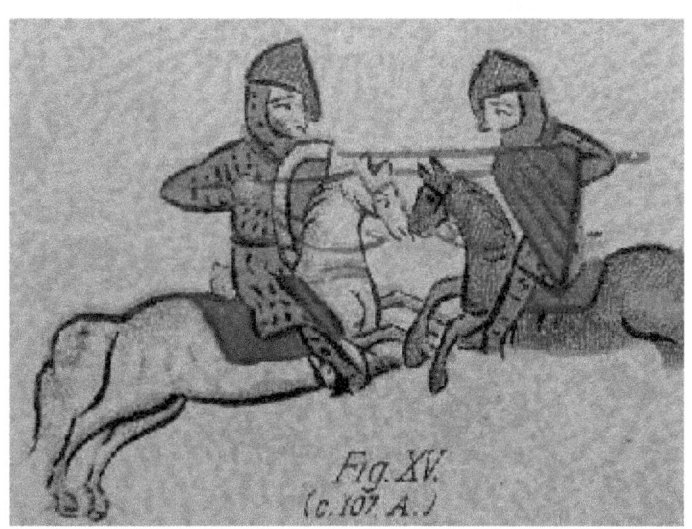

Annales, Tav. II, Fig. 15.

Annales, Tav. III, Fig. 16.

Appendix

Annales, Tav. III, Fig. 17.

Annales, Tav. IV, fig. 25.

Appendix

Annales, Tav. VI, fig. 33.

Annales, Fig: Tav. VI, fig. 34.

Appendix

Annales, Tav. VII, fig. 35.

Annales, Tav. VIII, fig. 37.

ABOUT THE AUTHOR

AGOSTINO INGUSCIO is Lecturer in Economic History and convenor of the MA programme in Economic History at the Department of Historical Studies of the University of Cape Town (SA).

He joined the University of Cape Town in 2014 after having been a postdoctoral fellow in Economic History at the Economic Growth Center of Yale University.

At UCT Agostino is developing the Economic History curriculum offered, by bringing to the students his experience relative to the long run drivers in economic history.

To support the growth of a graduate research community at the University of Cape Town, Agostino has been working towards the establishment of a research programme in Global Economic History.

The aim of the Global Economic History programme is to use its strategic position at the Cape to create cultural links and networks within the Global South. This is often perceived as an emerging reality, frequently conquering headlines. History however reveals how the process of connectedness has deep roots. The history of South Africa is global and we can only understand it in connection with the history of the other countries in Southern Africa, Africa and different continents.

The movement of people, goods and capital created the reality that we inhabit today. These three components of global connectivity however operated and flowed differently. The penetration capabilities of capital often dictated the agenda of people and goods.

Agostino's interest in moving to the University of Cape Town was also to broaden his geographical experience and to add to his knowledge in the economic history field from a developing country context.

He has always had a keen interest in the economic history of developing regions, which he cultivated during his period at the United Nations Department of Economic and Social Affairs in New York. Since spending a semester working there during his doctoral studies in 2010, Agostino has always kept in mind the current importance of our work as economic historians for the contemporary world.

Agostino Inguscio received a BA in Medieval History from the University of Florence (2006), as well as a Master of Science (2008) and a DPhil (2013) in Economic History from the University of Oxford.

Visit us at *www.quidprobooks.com*.

www.ingramcontent.com/pod-product-compliance
Lightning Source LLC
Chambersburg PA
CBHW072202160426
43197CB00012B/2486